To Marge
and
Fran — your
to increase your
delight at your
beach house!
Kathleen O'Be

MW00736947

LIFE IS A BEACH!

MUSINGS FROM THE SEA

Kathleen P. O'Beirne
Lifescape Enterprises

Other Works by the Author:

Pass It On! *How to Thrive in the Military Lifestyle*
ISBN 1-879979-00-4

Pass It On, II: *Living and Leaving the Military Lifestyle*
ISBN 1-879979-00-4

Student Passport
ISBN 1-879979-06-3

Mobile Student Passport
ISBN 1-879979-07-1

Birds of a Feather: *Lessons from the Sea*
ISBN 1-879979-02-0

Copyright © 2006 by Kathleen P. O'Beirne

Published by:
Lifescape Enterprises
P. O. Box 218
West Mystic, CT 06388

All rights reserved, including the right to reproduce this book or portions thereof in any form or by any means, electronic, or mechanical, including photocopying, recording, or by any information storage and retrieval system, without permission in writing from the author. All enquiries should be addressed to Lifescape Enterprises, P. O. Box 218, West Mystic, CT 06388

Printed in the United States of America

10 9 8 7 6 5 4 3 2

First Edition

Graphic Design by Jeanne Sigel

ISBN 1 –879979-09-8

PROLOGUE

*I am packing to leave my island. What have I for my efforts,
for my ruminations on the beach? What answers or solutions
have I found for my life?*

Anne Morrow Lindbergh,
Gift from the Sea, 1955

In the decade-plus that my husband and I have visited Sanibel
Island, Florida, for vacation periods, I have found myself musing on
issues that were challenging in my workplace, volunteer places, or
family relationships. I seemed to be able to find clarity there as I
walked the beach by myself for hours at a time. Distance in time,
space, and emotional involvement, plus the soothing motion of the
waves and their eradication of most other sounds gave me "gifts
from the sea."

As Anne Morrow Lindbergh learned half a century ago, there
are lessons we can translate from the world of nature to our
human arenas. While she focused on the stages of life, my lessons
here have more to do with the choices we make as we recruit,
retain, and reward folks in our workplace, and how these same
principles apply where we live, play, and volunteer.

Ten years of leadership in a human services organization taught
me how important our behaviors, intentions, and choices are.
When a group of thirty people serve thousands of people (and
provide multiple services for most), then it is critical that leadership
provides the wisest support possible for these usually over-
extended caregivers. Their reservoirs of well-being must be fairly
full in order for them to draw upon their resources for others.

A lifetime of leadership in volunteer organizations, with
recognition on the national level for that work, has also given me
vantage points for observation and experimentation. People are
involved in such work primarily because of the mission and what
they themselves garner from their efforts. Therefore, leadership
skills may be even more important in these settings where the
bottom line may not be monetary, but certainly is dependent upon
the goodwill of those who are free to choose their commitments.

A third setting in which a lot of my experimentation with creativity occurred was a senior research and development center for the U. S. Navy. Focused on cutting edge technology for submarines, this center was at risk for diminishing morale and productivity. My role as public affairs officer gave me a latitude to look at internal, as well as the traditional external affairs. With the interest and encouragement of my officer-in-charge, I began offering some lunch-time study series in conjunction with the National Endowment for the Humanities, who saw us as an "under-served population."

As these study series had remarkable success across all strata of the laboratory, I hatched the idea of a series on creativity, using the resident experts. With the support and collaboration of the technical director emeritus, a 13-week curriculum was developed. Excitement ran so high that even two concurrent sessions could not accommodate all who signed up.

Co-workers would poke their heads into our meeting room, curious as to the source of laughter and humpback whale songs. A senior scientist struggled to share the processes that took him from Beethoven's *Ninth Symphony* to his current sonar project. Once I saw the Escher morph graphic in his office, I was able to help him translate his process in yet another medium.

One of the most popular exercises was to explore our "R & D center" as a playground (or an airport or a grocery store). Pursuing metaphors to their limits yielded incredible results. This book explores the beach as a metaphor for the workplace, the family, and the volunteer place. Because our interactions with co-workers and clients/customers make great differences in our own quality of life, that of others, and the measurable success of our joint endeavors, please think deeply about the implications of nature's lessons – lessons from the sea.

Kathleen Parker O'Beirne
Mystic, Connecticut
2006

How to Use This Book: The Beach as Muse

I suggest reading this book in small portions, just as it was written, allowing time to muse and mull on the implications for your own life. There are enough sections to savor one a week with a few "snacks" in between.

Another option is to take it when you are traveling and have blocks of time to ponder. Dog-ear the ones you like best and want to revisit. You may choose to use some of the metaphors for staff training or a retreat.

As you muse, query at least three general domains:

Your personal or family life.

Your income-producing domain (which many call "work" or "job") and your volunteer connections.

All can benefit from a new angle of vision. Consistency in your approach across all three domains strengthens your likelihood of using new strategies productively.

I have often wished for wider margins in books, because some, like Anne Morrow Lindbergh's *Gifts from the Sea*, cry out for participatory reading. When I re-read my favorites, I use a different colored pen each time so I can see how my marginalia has changed in content and in depth of insight.

When Anne Morrow Lindbergh wrote, "Life is not a beach," she recognized that we neither can nor should live our lives fully in the contemplative mode. But, we need the contemplative time in order to return to our daily lives with energy renewed and insights deepened. Metaphors are useful triggers.

Perhaps you will "pass it on." Give copies to your friends, family, and co-workers. Your follow-on discussions could take a book club to a whole new dimension!

Contents

BEACHSCAPE AS LIFESCAPE!

Beachscape
as a Lifescape

It is important to select a metaphor for musing that will be coherent and cohesive. It should be a complete microcosm that can be translated symbolically en toto. Then, even seemingly inconsequential elements will help to flesh out the whole picture.

When we examine the beach as a total environment, we are reminded to look at not only the star specimens, but also at the Cormorant pellets, the Sponges, and the ugly Pen Shells. Just as we simply do not see key elements of our own lives, we miss the clues in our metaphorical beachscape. Hopefully, these musings will help us to focus on the importance and impact of the interdependencies and connections we find in a natural setting.

Although we rarely see the crabs that scurry over the beach at night or at least when we are not there, what signs let us know of their presence?

On a personal level, what are some of your unseen and unexamined attitudes and habits?

On a workplace level, what are some of the "givens" in your business culture?

If someone is new to you or to your workplace, how much is unknown and for how long?

Life as a Shell Mirror

Throughout these musings, I will use shells as a metaphor for people. Making decorative frames for mirrors has become both an artistic endeavor for me and a gift for friends and relatives. I have even taught classes, sharing my delight with adults and children old enough to use a glue gun safely. Quite remarkably, there have been no ugly frames or wreaths, and very few burned fingers!

Usually, participants bring some of their own shells that they have collected on their travels and have wanted to use in a way that they could enjoy them, rather than relegating them to a box on a shelf. They also relish discovering new shells from my Sanibel Island collections.

As we work, people who have not known each other before the class quickly forget their usual social fears. Children become equal creators with those older chronologically, because all are trying something new. They offer each other advice, share shells (because the supply is ample), and delight in each other's vision.

When all are done, the final step is an offer to spray each frame with clear shellac. That brings out the natural color that the shells had when they were wet on the seashore, and seals in any residual scent — especially important for Sea Whips (like a coral grass), Sea Grasses, and Crab claws that add so much character to their creation. Their awe is second only to mine, as they see themselves through their work. If they have done a mirror, they literally see themselves surrounded by their choices.

Our lives are like that, but how often do we stop to peer in the mirror at ourselves and also look intently at the frame that we have designed (by many choices and chances). I believe that if we learn to be more intentional about our choices and recognize chances for positive choices, then our lives will be more pleasing creations.

As you peer intently at your own life, what are its components? As you look at your workplace, what shells and sea creatures do you find there? Is there a design to your life (or workplace), or do you see just a jumble of collected items (attitudes, relationships, projects, and policies)?

Reflection

Reflection needs to be two-fold: to look at what one sees in the mirror and to ponder what meaning it holds. Our focus needs to be external and internal.

Whom do I see?
Who or what surrounds me?
Are changes desired?
If so, why? Which ones and how? When?

Although this exercise is done at some level several times a day, how frequently do we need a deeper and longer look? Because it is unlikely that we can take off for the beach for an extended vacation every several months, what else can we do?

Many find that during periods of exercise, such as walking, jogging, or swimming, their mind is freed for other pursuits.

If you live in an area where you have safe access to a natural area for hiking, boating, or taking a pet for a walk, this may provide a longer period for reflection. So, also, may an art museum or an evening of music that triggers introspection. Prayer and meditation are good options.

Directed dreaming is yet another strategy for quiet reflection at the end of the day.

What pursuits or strategies do you know
for enabling the double insights desired?

Unless You Get Out
and Walk Around...

If you simply observe the small portion of the beach that is close to you, you will have no idea what the broader environment is like on any given day. You must get out and look at other segments to know what is available and what is missing.

Failure to analyze methodically and frequently will cause myopia.

How often do you walk around your own beach?

How often do you scan other beaches (either by physically visiting them or reading about them)?

When you travel, do you choose sites that might enhance your business? Your creativity?

SELECTION OF SHELLS

Choosing Shells on the Beach

Just as in life, some people walk the beach picking up very few shells, if any. Some are either so focused on their exercise regimen or on the music/message from their earphones, that they do not notice the people or the shells that they pass. They could be anywhere; this specific environment makes little or no impact on them.

Others want only the biggest shells they can find, regardless of their inherent beauty (or lack thereof).

Some select only perfect specimens; they rarely need to have a bag to carry their treasures because they are so few and far between – even on a beach known for its remarkable volume and variety.

Some collect one shell of each type, often using an identification chart as a guide. This strategy resembles a game of Bingo, where all species are present and accounted for. A variation on this strategy is to keep upgrading as a more perfect specimen is found, tossing the lesser version.

Yet other shellers seem to have a project in mind, which they use as the basis for their choices. Even though there may be a plethora of Calico Scallops or Figs, these do not fit their plan and they pass them by.

Those who are purely acquisitive select their shells by whatever strikes their eye.

If we behave in these same ways as we choose members for our team in the workplace, what are the results?

How do you choose friends?

How do you choose employees?

How do you choose projects?

How do you lead your life?

Shell Identification

There are those who resist classifying people, believing that it is inappropriate to narrow complex creatures to types. However, we do that throughout nature. Current research on human personality typologies continues to prove that most of us become a core type by adolescence and make only minor variations on the theme over a lifetime.

Within each species, there are almost endless variations by age, size, environment of origin, current environment, coloration, etc. However, a Whelk is a Whelk, large, small, gold, burgundy, blue-gray, or gray-white. Recognizing the characteristics of each species takes experience and a desire to learn. The laminated identification charts are very helpful for those learning their shells, birds, and fish – in all weather! Much like the lifetime bird list that avid birders maintain, we could annotate our lifetime shell (or people) index.

But, with people, there is a next step for some of us. If we can identify them, how do we best interact with them? Will they be suitable for our enterprise? Are they keepers? Do we seek them out or pass them by? Or, more actively, do we avoid or reject them?

How do you identify potential friends?

How do you identify potential employees?

*Do you actively seek them or
do you wait for them to pass by?*

IQ vs. EQ

At first, the sheer volume of shell species seems overwhelming and we wonder if we need to be a genius to memorize the names and shapes of all of them. The identification chart from our cottage complex shows 56 local specimens that are commonly found in the region. Naturally, we learn most quickly the ones we see most often. We remember them for the duration of the trip; but, we need memory-refreshment the next time around.

I have used this chart with fourth graders each spring as they put their book learning to the hands-on test. They circle their seven or eight "must-finds" and then delight in identifying the other random treasures.

What matters more than cognitive skills, according to all who have looked at the issue deeply, is our passion to learn and to share what we have discovered. Unfortunately, most elementary school training accentuates the classification portion of intelligence, but fails to demonstrate and nurture the emotional quotient (EQ) that has a far greater impact on our lives. When I share my newest shell mirror with the class and then read a poem about the shells, I share on a higher level – and to my amazement, the students follow suit by sending me their own poems a week later!

"Inspect what you expect." This old management adage underscores the technical, sequential, document-your-work mentality that is too limited for our era of change, flexibility, adaptability, and vision.

"Honor and nurture" might be a better motto for today. People live and work more productively in environments in which they feel safe, valued, and excited. We must all learn how to do this better.

What do you feel passionate about?

How are you able to share this?

What are the rewards? For you?
For others?

Beach Reverse

I find it fascinating that under normal circumstances I am the "glue" in social relations in our home community. However, when I get to Sanibel Island, I have expectations that free me from other than the perfunctory "Hello's" on the beach.

Meanwhile, my usually introverted spouse makes special connections with "the fisher ladies" and others who overlap our annual segment. He becomes quite gregarious and chats with an assortment of folks who gather at the beach Tiki Hut to celebrate the sunset. What's going on?

On closer inspection there really isn't such an apparent change in perspective. He engages folks on a short-term basis and protects his long-term privacy. I do the reverse – my tendency to accumulate a vast array of wonderful people is temporarily put in abeyance to give me the quiet, uninterrupted time I so desperately need.

We are a pair! (47 years worth of pair, including many years of submarine duty that took him away for more than half of each year).

How do you change off with a key partner?

Where Do I Look?

Most of us believe that if we have found one special shell in a specific location, that there will be more in the same spot. However, this is generally not true. Wave action disperses even colonial creatures quite far and wide. Unlike one's experiences ashore, where it is reasonable to expect that when one finds a certain kind of rock, there will be others nearby .... on the beach, shells and other marine life have been churned up by waves and deposited randomly.

More generically, one can count on finding certain species or sizes on different beaches. For example, when I want some small "tuckers," those little shells that fill the gaps left by the larger shells when I am making a shell wreath, I head to the beach at Captiva. There I find mostly small species (such as Augers and Coquinas) and immature versions of the larger species. The scale of the shells is small to "shell hash" well on its way to becoming sand. It is easier to spot the tiny specimens when they are not competing with larger treasures.

So, it does pay to look for certain sizes in different environments. But, I will not expect to find another Junonia in exactly the same location today or any other day. That means I must always be alert to finding a treasure anywhere at any time.

Do you have favorite stores for different items?

Have you been surprised to find a treasure "out of place" — i.e., not in the situation or setting where you would have expected it?

Have you found people who are treasures in unexpected places?

Do you always find a treasure every time you return to a given setting?

13

Find a Star?
Look Next Door

Often when one sights a particularly interesting bird or shell, the tendency is to zero in on the stellar attraction. Interestingly enough, there is often another star in the neighborhood.

In the case of birds, a Green Heron or an even-rarer Bittern will perch just inside the foliage next to a Small Blue Heron or a Tri-colored Heron. This is by choice. This is symbiosis and often takes place in the workplace where a less flashy "star" will feel blessed with the attention a gregarious star brings to the team.

Shells are by chance — but a narrow focus can cause one to miss a very interesting, perhaps less colorful shell nearby.

Do you know of such pairings?

What does each bring to the other?

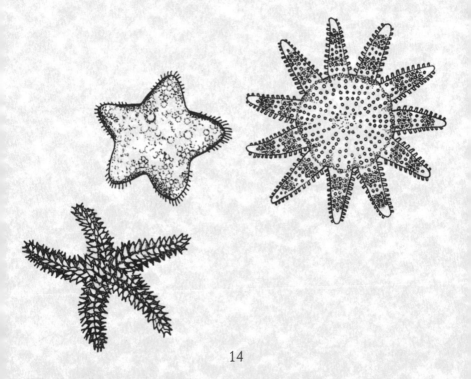

Variety by Design

As I have created a number of shell mirrors and wreaths over the years (and a number of teams in workplace and volunteer settings), I have discovered that variety is usually more effective than a creation with only one or two specimens predominating. This is true for a number of reasons:

One is that small shells are needed to fill in the gaps left by the larger shells;

Second, variety adds texture and depth to the design. Just as the shells overlap on the seashore, those placed in tandem with other species remind the viewer of their differences;

Third, coloration is more noteworthy when there are other colors and shapes for comparison. While I do sometimes create an all-white mirror, or one that plays with hues of peach, melon, and orange, then the stimulus must be the variety of species. Otherwise, it would be boring in its sameness.

You may have seen commercial shell wreaths that are the equivalent of paint-by-the-number. A row of identical Scallops rings the outside, all face down. Then, a row of Clams rings the inside. On the top, a sprinkling of Cowries (not random, by any means) completes these very durable, very unimaginative productions. In a one-version-suits-all spirit, these patterns find their way to hotel room walls, intent on filling an allotted space. If one were damaged, not to worry – it can be replaced exactly by another in the storeroom.

While some corporations and franchises do attempt to quantify and qualify their teams in just such a manner, so the replacement factor is guaranteed, most settings to which we gravitate as employees and volunteers provide more leeway for differences and the positives that come with pride in our uniquenesses.

When I teach shell wreath classes, I urge participants to search out non-shell material as well: sea glass, Crab backs and claws, feathers, seeds, pieces of coral, grasses that will dry between newspapers, Whelk cases (those curly bands of pods from which the baby Whelks emerge before the "skin" is washed up on the shore), and lacy collections of Banded Tulip eggs. Their comments at first indicate that they have never seen any shell mirrors with these items included. When done, they recognize how much personality and whimsy comes with these additions.

All of us would benefit by adding personal touches and fun to our work places. That way we get to know and express ourselves more fully and have the opportunity to gain insights about others.

Have you enjoyed the opportunity to visit a doctor or dentist who has enriched his or her often-sterile environment? How about the mobiles or art on the ceiling in your dental hygienist's office or the seasonal hot pads adorning the cold steel foot stirrups in the gynecologist's office? Your visit is immediately changed from the often frightening, bad-news-is-expected scenario to one in which you can expect a warm, personal, and professional interface.

Likewise, the hygienist and gynecologist are more likely to enjoy their work setting and their rapport with patients. Studies of work sites, hospitals, schools, and congregate-living for elderly folks have all found that personal expression enhances the quality and quantity of the product or services delivered and improves the consumption by the customers.

What personal and whimsical touches have you added to your home décor? To your menu?

What personal and whimsical touches have you added to your workplace?

If you are a supervisor, what freedoms of expression could you encourage to enhance the delight and productivity of your staff and customers?

Variety
in Recruitment

When it is time to recruit a whole new team or to find the appropriate "replacement" for an employee who has left an existing group, the temptation may be to look for exactly the same kind of people or person. However, this is an opportunity to create a new work of art, even if you are selecting only one shell.

It would be easy just to look for another Scallop shell (same size, same color); but, try out a piece of Coral, a Jingle, or a couple of Cats Paws. The new configuration may give new life to the whole frame.

When you are in-filling, the successor needs to be compatible with those already in place, but that does not mean identical in size, color, or texture to the predecessor or those around the vacancy. This is an opportunity to promote new interfaces with the existing members as well as with the newcomer.

When a whole new mirror frame is called for, it is a chance to examine its purpose and research the variety of options that exist. Maybe you could collect new specimens from a different beach or two. It is natural to choose some of your tried-and-true favorites, but consider an array of sizes, ages, species, and genders.

Genders, you say? Well, maybe not quite, but many folks do not know that the very colorful Calico Scallop shells at Sanibel Island have two different sides. While one side of the pair has a busy rose-colored pattern, the other side may sport a rose band around a totally white shell. They are chromatically synchronized, their shapes are identical, but their patterns are dissimilar.

Age, you say? Sometimes the very tiny, young shells are more likely to be free of fractures, barnacles, and holes drilled by predators. On the other hand, even fragments of more mature shells have such amazing character that you can incorporate them in your design by showing their best side.

Although we all have a predilection for certain styles of behavior, selection of a few different patterns or colors can make the difference between the mundane and the remarkable combination. Have the courage to try!

If you could select your ideal temporary committee for a special task, what would it look like? If, for example, you wanted to fill a pastoral search committee for your church as it seeks a new minister, what would be key varieties you would seek to recruit?

What project(s) do you have in the workplace that would benefit from an ad hoc group to come together to work temporarily?

What benefits do you see in this arrangement?

Value of Shells

As I was walking further up the beach than usual yesterday, a young couple approached me with a query. Folks do that at Sanibel Island. There is a freedom from the usual protocols, probably based on the common denominator of the awe of the beach.

The young man asked, "So, which are the really expensive shells?" I paused at the unexpected perspective and then answered, "The ones you <u>aren't finding</u>! But, do you know which are the really fun shells?" He looked puzzled and his wife chuckled before I could answer, "The ones you <u>are finding</u>!"

I saw them again later when we had all reversed directions, and they gave a big smile and a wave. They obviously had had a chance to think about our interchange and were at least amused by my response.

How do we appraise the value of something or someone?

How does pleasure with what we have counter the desire for what we don't have?

What leadership lessons are here?

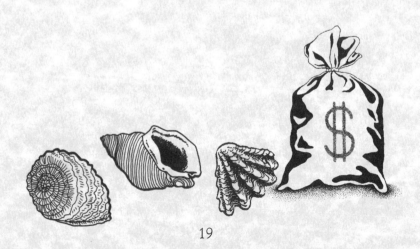

19

Changed Perspective

Most of us unconsciously prefer gaining our information through the same side of our brain. We sit in church, at a movie theater, or in a lecture in the same general location. Those who sit on the right as they listen are processing the preacher's words through their left brain (their logical-sequential brain). Those who choose to sit on the left receive their information through their right brain (their global-aesthetic brain). Of course, the ideal is to be able to use whichever side of the brain is most suited to the task at hand.

If you walk on the beach at mid-day (no shadows), try walking the same strip twice – once with the shells on your left side and once on the right. I guarantee that you will select different items. Your left brain can be tasked to look for specific species and it will do so efficiently. But, your left brain also gets tricked easily. If it has just seen a rare flat version of a Scallop, it will see more of the same because it logically connects the desired with the actual more common types at hand.

Your right brain will be drawn to the artistic elements on the beach and is open to finding things it has not been programmed for.

As an experiment, put your written notes to the left of your computer and write a short essay. Then try the right side. As a journalist, I use this strategy depending on what outcome I want.

Try sitting in different locations for regular staff meetings. You will read body language better with your right brain. For specific, detailed tasking assignments, your left brain is better equipped to grasp the structure – especially from a left-brained boss.

When searching for an idea or solution, try looking up to the left for awhile. Then, try looking up to your right. To connect the thoughts, look straight ahead.

20

More Selective
Over Time

Folks who are brand new to the beach in general or those who are newly returned to a given beach will tend to pick up more shells at first. They worry about quantity more than quality. They may worry that weather, tides, storms, or weeds might impact the shells' availability in the future.

Later in their stay, once assured of an adequate supply, they become more selective. One would usually say "discriminating" (except for its negative workplace connotation). More discerning. Perhaps the shortness of their stay and the challenge of adding any more to their baggage is operating at a conscious or subconscious level.

So, too, when starting up a new office or team, the urge to fill the positions may cause one to be less selective than you will be later when you must in-fill just one employee.

Are you new on the beach?

Is your space limited?

Are you usually cautious or expansive by nature?

Are you usually acquisitive vs. Spartan in your choices?

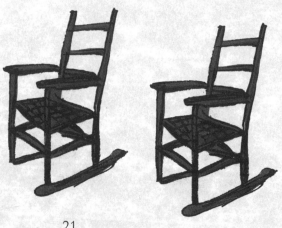

Am I Good Enough?

Are the last shells best? Toward the end of my annual visit to Sanibel Island, I am forced by my own sense of surfeit and my daily reminder of the accumulating collection of treasures on our porch, that I must limit any more acquisitions. They must be superior to join my already remarkable collection.

As members of your team see the newest hires, they sometimes wonder if they would have made the cut now. What they are not factoring into their comparison is their own performance since coming aboard.

In actuality, because they have become more remarkable in your setting, they have upped the ante for compatible new hires. How can you let them know this in order to head off misperceptions that could damage their continued growth and diminish the acclimatization of the new hires?

On a personal level, have you felt diminished by someone you've met?

How did you handle your self-talk?

Would the person you encountered be surprised by your reaction?

Could you be productive partners?

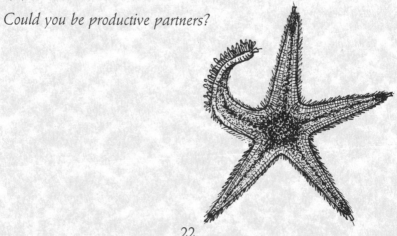

Observe, Witness, and Admire

There are times to simply admire what someone else has built or collected. Without envy, we can observe, witness, and admire.

For example, there are shells far too large for our endeavors that appear on the beach or in shops for sale. They are remarkable and teach us about the abstract level of beauty and excellence. However, our reaction should be awe, not envy. We should look for lessons, not ownership.

At Sanibel Island, there are accommodations that have incredible vistas and architectural beauty. Far from envying those homeowners, I hope that they are frequently in residence and that they relish and share the joy of their vistas.

The same attitude is important in aspects of our workplace, volunteer setting, or family. Rather than feeling diminished by the unique accomplishments of others and, therefore, envious, we should exult in their "one step for all mankind." While not all endeavors are of this magnitude, the magnanimity of John Glenn is a model to emulate.

Are there specimens that you admire?

How do you cope with the natural tendency to envy?

*Are you the object of envy?
If so, how can you deal
with it positively?*

There's Always a New Wave

Even though you are walking a beach you have walked many times before, and may even have walked earlier on this very day, you will be blessed with changed conditions. Most of all, the wave action pushing in and retreating lays bare a brand new beach many times per minute.

You could just sit in one place and watch the variations in your own little microcosm. Sometimes that is all that we have the physical, mental, or social energy to accomplish. At other times, you may stride confidently, observing the macrocosm and periodically checking the micro.

Even though others are walking just ahead of you or are coming toward you, do not despair. They will have looked with different eyes at different angles and you will have the new waves.

Most of us have a tendency to forget that every moment brings us an opportunity to see anew or be different. It takes courage and mindfulness to live so intently in the present.

Of the three tenses, which do you favor? The Past?
The Present? The Future? We need all three in balance.

What insights come to you from the Past?
The Present? The Future?

What leadership lessons come from the wave action
and the variety of points of view?

Try a New Beach
(or walk further on this one)

"There are no shells!" While that is <u>never</u> literally true at Sanibel Island, the whiner is complaining about the perceived lack of "collector shells." Because s/he is so focused on the large or trophy shells, s/he misses the Coquinas. Coquinas are the bright little purple, lavender, pink, and yellow bi-valves highly prized by the red-legged White Ibis. They have a delicate sunrise pattern and can be lovely in small arrangements.

Are you feeling bored or disenchanted with your situation? Would a change of location bring stimulation and a new perspective? Sometimes, you may find that you really need to pick up your sand bucket and move to a completely different beach, where at least if things are not better, they are not the same. A whole new beach might be joining a business or professional organization, or it might be seeking a new job.

At other points in your ennui or discomfort, simply going further on your current beach may provide the new perspective you are seeking. It is amazing how different stretches of the same beach can be. So, a lateral change may make all of the difference. For example, your church may offer two or three different worship options: the Saturday evening gospel/informal version; the early Sunday service that focuses on the message or communion; and the traditional main service with the choir and social interaction at the end. Choosing a new service would mean seeing people you usually miss and your worship might have a new flavor.

In our businesses and workplaces, we must learn to be as flexible and opportunistic as the shorebirds. Each wave brings a new beach. If your beach seems consistently barren, find a new beach!

What change(s) could you make personally that would bring you stimulation and delight? (You deserve delight!!)

What change(s) could you make for yourself in your workplace?

What opportunities for change could you support for others in your workplace?

What opportunities exist (or could be created) in your workplace to draw employees from across the spectrum for special projects? Remember the study series I mentioned in the Prologue? We drew folks across the departments and across the hierarchies – they came for lunch and discussion on specific topics, and were fed beyond their wildest dreams. And once fed, they were determined not to let go of the opportunity!

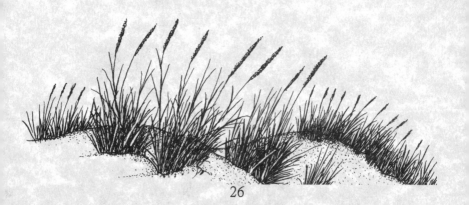

Compatibility

After the end of her first week on the job, I heard our newest staff member commenting on how well everyone got along. She had been badly "damaged" in her prior job and was puzzled about "why does comfort reign here?"

"Do you think that the boss actually chooses people who will work well together?" The lead secretary who heard this query was startled that it seemed like such a radical concept (or luxury) to the new employee. But, the truth is that many workplaces and volunteer agencies need people so desperately that they accept whoever comes their way. While it is short-sighted in the long haul, it fills slots in the short term.

When selectivity is applied to newcomers, and coaching, support, and training are provided to those already in place, a healthy turnover can be accomplished fairly quickly.

Compatibility plus social glue can result in a very handsome wreath. The leader must take the risk of stopping an old dysfunctional pattern and consciously choosing a new paradigm.

Do you need to make paradigm changes in your family?

Do you need to make paradigm changes in your work place or volunteer setting?

How do you recognize the newcomer who craves a healthy setting and then provide the support s/he needs to become acclimated to and productive in your remarkable environment?

How do you enable your current staff to appreciate and perpetuate your remarkable environment?

Choosing Your Workplace Palette

Because I've worked predominantly in the human services field, I sought employees who were bright in coloration, capable of holding the attention of the workshop audiences to whom they presented information, and capable of energizing those who felt overwhelmed by life's challenges. I wanted the best and brightest available on the beach.

I can understand that other settings might call for a different mix. As managers hire and as employees seek to be hired, both need to look carefully at the fit in the palette.

On a personal level, what palette is your favorite?
(A peek in your closet might be a clue.)

Do you crave excitement and creativity,
or would a calmer, predictable setting
be your preference?

In your workplace, do you need quietly
capable people or those with more energy
and panache? Or a mix of both?

Look on the Inside and Outside

Some of the ugliest exteriors hide lovely interiors. The Atlantic Wing is a dark, crusty, asymmetrically shaped shell that has an exquisite mother-of-pearl lining. The Venus Clam has a dense outer shell with a few un-noteworthy patterns. However, the inside may be a deep purple, rose, gold, or orange. While the outside may have drill burrows, the inside may show no sign of predation.

Some shells show their colors all of the way through. The Buttercup Lucina and the Dosinia are almost translucent in their appearance. You can forecast the hidden side by what you see.

When selecting shells for your project, you can afford to choose some for one attribute or profile only. If you must work with fewer shells or place them in a highly visible setting, those who pass the 360-degree assessment offer greater flexibility and credibility.

Do you personally enjoy knowing a lot of different people?
Do you choose certain folks for certain activities?
Do you sing with some and shop with others?
Walk with one and do creative projects with another?

How hard is it to get to know another "inside?"

How does it happen in a workplace?

How does it happen in an interview?

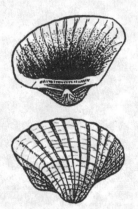

They Warm the Cockles of My Heart

One finds very large brown and tan striped shells that are most unspectacular on the outside. However, their colorfully striped insides are marvels to behold. Even fragments are beautiful in their own right. They are named "Heart Cockles" because of the shape they form where the bi-valves come together on the inside. Their ridges curve in a heart shape and the coloration at this juncture can be brilliant reds and golds.

They are larger than most of the shells on the beach and often wind up as ashtrays. The careful observer will value their inner beauty.

In the workplace, there is a similar phenomenon....the worker whose outward appearance gives little evidence of the mind, heart, or soul hidden within.

How often is size part of our value judgment of an individual?

How often is a drab exterior a put-off?

Do you know any "ashtrays?"

Do we think about our carrying capacity when choosing to leave these shells behind? If so, how do we define "carrying capacity?"

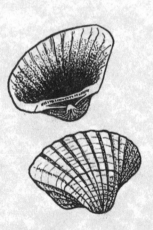

Collect Wherever You Go

Once you become a shell seeker, you will probably find yourself looking at new places with a different eye. While some countries forbid the importation or exportation of shells, many do not.

I am always surprised when visitor documents ask my occupation. Years ago, when I was a teacher, I was carefully queried by customs officials whether I intended to remain and teach. I was just a tourist, but puzzled by the intent of the entry inspector's questions. In later years, I discovered that "journalist" was another hot button, even though that was an honest answer as to my occupation. I find myself safer with "retired civil servant" these days; but, who knows, some may expect the CIA!

Wherever I travel for training or consulting, I always have my eye out for exceptional people who could become part of my network for current and future projects. Scan the beach wherever you go (and know that the reverse is probably happening).

Has your profile raised questions in formal settings?

If so, what do you think has been behind the seemingly unusual interest?

Have you found unusual talents or ideas in places you have visited for vacation, conferences, or inspection trips?

Have you been successful in "collecting" these exceptional specimens?

*P.S. I am so "bad" (avid) about collecting shells that once I noticed a bank parking lot in Georgia had been covered in dredge material (the seaside equivalent of gravel). There were Miocene Era fossils (26 million years old) serving as road surface.
I was on my knees!

31

Quality

Often when we are surrounded by a beach of incredible shells, it is hard to maintain some inner measure of their quality in the world beyond this site. My staff often would listen with only half an ear when I sang their praises. Believing that I was a cockeyed optimist and perpetual cheerleader rolled into one, they did not believe in their own stature until they had the opportunity to go to other sites for training conferences with their worldwide counterparts. Once exposed to their cohorts, they had a way to measure their own absolute quality vs. just their relative value among exceptional individuals in our center.

There comes a time when it is important to understand our standing in our field of endeavor. We may then have the added opportunity to model the ideal and train others in our specific areas of excellence, while seeking out the same where we want to improve. One star employee, in assessing the value of a particular training, commented that no one else seemed to be offering the kinds of developmental programming that was our norm, and therefore, she had not gotten very much out of the expensive experience... Time to mentor! Quality does matter... on a daily basis.

Have you experienced this phenomenon of being at the head of the pack and being distressed by it?

Why is that a threatening (or disappointing) experience?

What strategies can you use to mentor others while still gaining new and valuable information/initiatives for your own setting?

Does Collette Dowling's "Cinderella complex" have validity here?

After remembering Dr. Mary Bunting's studies on the fear of success among female Harvard MBA and law school students, reassess your own motivation and mission.

Envision, Seek, and Ye Shall Find

After a big storm, the beach was littered with soft sea grasses and Pen Shells, but also with my favorite Sea Whips, which are coral grasses. As I was excitedly collecting the purple and yellow coral grasses, a man coming toward me had a handful of the purple. I commented that he was one of few I had ever seen picking them up and he told me how he used them. He has lived on the beach for many years, but he was amazed to see my yellow ones!

As I walked on in the area from which he had just come, I found four more yellow Sea Whips in about five minutes. It does matter what you have asked your eyes and brain to search for, because they are then programmed for these items, should they be available.

Another example from the same day was a woman proudly showing me the half of a Sea Biscuit that she had found (and said her sister had just found a whole one). Plain white and kind of puffy, the Sea Biscuit does not stand out in a crowd. In fact, it usually is broken in a crowd.

I had not even thought of Sea Biscuits until that moment. Later in the afternoon, one appeared on my radar! How many had I passed by simply because I was not looking for them? How many do I want?

Are there treasures that you need to envision so that you will have your antennae out? In your personal life? In your workplace?

What quantity would you want of such a treasure?

Why?

33

Luck?

Often people will attribute their success, whether it be shelling or at work, to luck. While I do believe that there is an element of good fortune in many of our accomplishments, I believe that the greater proportion comes from research, structure, and recognition of an opportunity when it presents itself.

At the beach, I can read the tide charts, have my collecting gear ready, set my alarm clock for just before dawn, get out on the beach promptly and head for the known sandbars and shell piles. At first, I don't see very clearly as the sun is not high enough to illumine anything other than a huge shell (and folks with flashlights usually have picked those up earlier). I frankly don't want a huge shell – live shelling is forbidden and a non-live large shell usually is much damaged.

Once the sun is up a little higher, and the birds have begun to visit the beach, I keep my eyes peeled. I usually have some specific things that I am looking for to use on a current project, but I am always open to the unusual or the beautiful. So, when I find many wonderful specimens each day, am I only lucky or has my preparation played a role in recognizing opportunities?

Being called "lucky" diminishes our involvement in the outcome of a project. Women particularly have difficulty in owning their efforts that have led to achievement, but are very ready to accept blame for mistakes. This is the "locus of control" phenomenon in which men more typically take credit for accomplishments, while disclaiming responsibility for negative results.

When have you been called "lucky?"
How did it feel?

What leadership lessons are to be learned about luck? For yourself?

For others with whom you work?

What is your personal balance between choice and chance?

34

Buying Shells

I guess I'm old-fashioned or a purist about finding my own shells. Part of the fun is the discovery itself, as well as knowing the origin.

There are some shells whose bright coloration would make you doubt their authenticity. The Pectin, a Scallop with just one "leg," comes in such a bright orange, purple, or yellow, that shell shops have signs that read, "Yes, this is their natural color. They have not been dyed!" If you found one on the beach, you would be more inclined to believe.

Buying shells (read hiring a "headhunter") leaves one with some uncertainties.

Were they legally obtained or raided?

Did they come from tainted waters?

Were they protected species whose loss will have long-term effects on their previous environment? Do I care? Why?

Are they potential misfits in my collection?

Will they be easily recruited by someone else once I spend time enhancing them?

Selectivity

Experienced beachcombers have developed a protocol to help them resist the temptations they encounter. Their first strategy is: before you head to the beach, look at what you already have. Note abundances and anticipated shortfalls for upcoming projects before you start your search.

The second best time to be selective is on the beach. Admire the shells, but do not pick them up if they do not fall in your categories of needed or exceptional. This takes great restraint.

The third best time is to compare those that you do select against what you already have back at the cabin. If they are no more special than those you have already "conditioned" (i.e., cleaned and sorted), or are not compatible, take them back to the beach (and release them randomly, rather than in one little pile that has your name on it!).

Once past these tests, go ahead and "condition" your shells. For shells that means bleach water and removal of any debris caught in the edges of the univalves (like Olives and Whelks). For people, it means newcomer orientation plus the requisite corporate training sessions. As training is provided, your increasing investment makes the decision to release them harder. The same is true for new friendships in which we invest time, intimacies, and trust.

How do we learn selectivity?

Why is it important in our personal and professional lives?

How do you keep your head (i.e., standards) when all about are losing or compromising theirs?

Symmetry vs. Asymmetry

Many prefer compositions in which there are identical components or redundancies. However, aestheticians favor asymmetry that keeps a design off-balance, providing visual and intellectual motion.

Asymmetry is both easier and more difficult than paint-by-the-numbers symmetry. It can be awful or quite scintillating. Study the experts for guidance. Look at the artists who have changed the norms of their era.

On the beach, there are often comments about wishing that one were more artistic in order to capture the beauty of the designs and fragments found. Those of us who are not gifted graphic artists may be gifted in our human endeavors.

How can we replicate the interplay of the vertical linear design on one side of a Conch Shell with the zigzag pattern adjacent to it? There is actually a growth line between the two patterns. What needs to be prescribed/proscribed in our workplace and what can be more flexible? How can these two patterns provide energy and excitement in our design?

Rules in workplaces tend to favor symmetry. What examples can you think of? Why are they important? When do they stifle?

What benefits could asymmetry bring to your workplace? What are several domains in which asymmetry could be possible (where one-of-a-kind vs. a balanced pair could not only be tolerated, but provide a quantum leap)?

Do you have a mix in your personal life of "constants" and flexibility?

CHALLENGES...

Challenging Shells

There are those shells whose scale, shape, or coloration make them difficult to accommodate in my design.

The large, dark, and surprisingly fragile Pen Shells are overwhelming in bulk. However, shards of their dark opalescent point can be quite lovely as accents. Very young Pen Shells are gossamer beige, but their fragility is challenging and requires care out of proportion to their potential contribution to a design.

The Zebra Ark, also known as a Turkey Wing, is very angular and often larger than amenable to my design. However, small ones or those with exceptional coloring can add nice counterpoint to other shapes.

Very black Scallop Shells or Jingles do stand out on the beach. If you have a specific project in mind working with grays and blacks, they will be stunning. Otherwise, they are jarring to a composition.

In a workplace scenario, they are most effective in teams of their own scale or as temporary additions or consultants. Because they stand out in any crowd, they should be "perfect." Perhaps individuals of this magnitude are best suited as solo performers in a variety of fields. Their visibility can be a marketing plus, but they will have to be good "up close and personal."

Have you experienced a large or small Pen Shell in your workplace or personal life?

Can you identify other challenging individuals and determine what settings might be appropriate for them?

Back to the issue of selectivity, should you leave these challenging shells on the beach rather than trying to adapt them to your setting (or vice versa)?

Fragments

While I do need some whole shells, and I must force myself to collect some perfect "usual" shells in order for the rest to stand out, I also cherish fragments. Fragments are to be valued for two reasons:

*they can be beautiful all by themselves –
they have aesthetic value;*

the mind's eye rounds out fragments to their complete version and one doesn't sense sadness for their lack of wholeness.

We can get carried away in our society demanding perfection and youth when, in truth, portions of a remarkable work should be recognized and supported – so that the performer has the emotional energy to continue. In the same vein, as our work force ages, there will be flashes of the extraordinary as authors and performers coalesce heretofore-unconnected pieces – pieces that may lead the way to quantum leaps.

Beauty and perfection leave most of our population out. Few are possessed of physical beauty and perfection. However, many have fragments that can make this a wonderful world.

I keep a dish of fragments on my desk to remind me. When I make a shell wreath, I place the fragments in such a way that the viewer sees them at their best. I think that this is what a good leader does for her staff.

What fragments do you possess that you value?

What fragments exist in your workplace that could be nurtured and valued?

How can you train your eye and mind to supply the magic beyond the fragment?

Using Fragments in Your Design

One year I took a bowl full of colorful fragments back to my staff who were still in the throes of a cloudy gray New England winter/spring (it's hard to tell where winter leaves off and spring truly begins in our neck of the woods!). I had shared perfect shells with them in other years and had talked about how exceptional they were – because even in a world-class setting like Sanibel Island, they stood out.

But, the fragments had a different lesson to teach. We were undergoing significant external challenges in our workplace and none of us felt perfect at that point. We felt grateful to be a fairly large chunk of our former selves. So, the message was to notice the beauty in even the fragments and what our brains do upon seeing them – they fill in the remainder of the shape!

While I would certainly not start out to create a new team made up entirely of fragments, I can use many of them profitably by positioning them very carefully. Particularly in the company of other whole specimens, which may not be as scintillating, they add value and visions of what they can be when whole.

In a human setting, those fragments, with lots of TLC and leadership skills, may become versions of their former selves.

Another concept to remember is that many of the shells on the beach were originally part of a pair that make up the whole bi-valve. Many workers bring only half of themselves to the workplace (and leave the other half at home or in a volunteer setting that brings them a sense of completion).

What lessons do fragments teach us, particularly during times of stress?

Does the bi-valve lesson have value for us in our various settings?

Angle of Light

At daybreak, when my husband and I first begin to walk the beach, it is hard for our eyes to distinguish anything unless it is very large or very bright. Gradually, as more light comes, our eyes are able to focus more definitively. Then, a period comes that always takes me by surprise and amuses me as the sun directly behind us casts our shadows ahead of us. We become our own impediments to vision.

Conversely, if one is walking toward the sunrise, this is a period of blinding light. The discomfort is palpable and the shells cast shadows on the beach, distorting their shapes.

Before too long, the sun ascends and permits a more usual angle of light....and yet, as we walk with the sun at our backs, we wonder how people coming toward us have missed some of the treasures in their path. The answer lies partly in the angle of light they experience as they walk into the rising sun. The Reddish Heron has a strategy to cope with this problem. He raises his wing and peers under it at the water. His portable sunshade permits him to peer beneath the surface.

When have you been blinded? In your personal life? In your business life?

Could a wing shading the light have been helpful in deciphering what was in the water?

How can you use a new angle of light to change your perspective positively? When would you choose to walk toward the sun and when away?

How does the lesson of timing impact your decision-making?

Cinnamon Algae

At times, everything on the beach is covered by a sprinkling of red. Whether "good" or "bad," this granular camouflage prevents me from seeing the shells accurately. Their coloration, age, and condition are obscured, for good or for ill. The next tide usually will remove the sprinkling, as will a simple rinsing of the shells.

Environmental impact on a whole workplace, family, or volunteer organization can operate in a similar fashion. A reality check can be a simple rinse in a separate environment. However, the "red tide" can be a highly toxic, persistent phenomenon that is not easily flushed away and leaves significant casualties – even manatees, at the top of the food chain, are endangered.

Friendships forged during the common experience of a crisis may not continue once the challenge has passed. Behaviors common to fraternity brothers may disappear when they disperse to new settings. The golden glow of a retreat weekend may be hard to maintain under the fluorescent lights on Monday morning.

What experiences have you had with fleeting change?

How did you determine the "real" coloration or behavior?

Is there a danger in high intensity settings such as retreats that encourage people to open up uncharacteristically and then do not provide the ongoing support for continued positive change?

Camouflage – how do you feel about a system-wide attempt to disguise?

The Enigmatic Slipper Shell

Almost without fail, when I spot a shell on the beach that I cannot identify, it is a Slipper Shell. It comes in many sizes, colorations, surface designs, and degree of curvature. The underside has a little kangaroo-like pouch, which gives it the appearance of a scuff-along slipper.

It seems to be the shell with one thousand faces, the camouflage artist of the beach. I must confess that I dislike being duped by this shell and do not add many, if any, to my creations.

In human terms, there are those who find slippery folks amusing and harmless. They find my aversion senseless and petty. I think slippery folks are energy and focus sappers.

Do you know people who are the equivalent of the Slipper Shell?

What characteristics do they have in common?

Are there things or processes that have an enigmatic or camouflage component?

What can you do to make early recognition more likely?

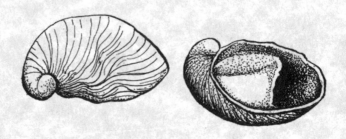

Fragile Shells

There are some shells, such as the Angel Wing, Fig, Sailor's Ear, and the Sea Biscuit, that are extremely thin. Some Jingles fall in this category as well. The Sand Dollar tends to crumble easily.

In order to carry such a specimen, I must decide either to devote a whole hand to it (thus precluding carrying another), or I must swath it in tissue and place it in my shirt pocket.

I treasure some of these for their inherent beauty, but also for the difficulty of finding a whole one and keeping it that way. Sometimes, several coats of clear spray shellac will toughen them enough to be handled.

In an organization or a family, how much attention can be devoted to fragile shells? If I am going to keep that shell with me, I can provide the tender loving care it needs; but, I would be reluctant to place it on a frame that I intend to part with. The issues of maintenance and potential breakage are too great.

Do you have any fragile shells in your family, workplace, or volunteer arena?

What do they add?

What do they "cost?"

What can we learn from them?

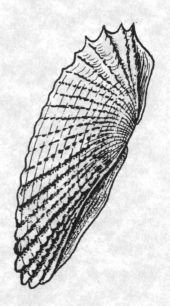

The Seemingly Fragile Shells

I am amazed to find that after two days of heavy winds and crashing waves, there are whole Sailor's Ear shells or Sea Urchins on the beach. They are very thin and usually are cracked or broken by the time they arrive.

Perhaps because they are light and have ridden high in the water, they have escaped unscathed.

Is that true of humans? In times of chaos, are those who travel lighter less burdened?

Is it possible that after a major upheaval, the floaters survive while other usually sturdy folks are damaged?

In corporate storms, mergers, downsizings, etc., are the buoyant lightweights more likely to survive?

If so, what are the consequences for
our collective beach?

Rose-Colored Glasses

Quite inadvertently, I bought a pair of rose-tinted dark glasses some years ago because I liked the frames. They quickly became my favorites, because the beach looked so wonderful. It took me awhile to figure out that the tint really was adding excitement to the hues on the beach; but, then I chose to wear them anyway, pausing periodically to do a reality check with my bare eyes when a specimen seemed too remarkable to believe.

I recommend them. Even on cloudy days, the world has a glow and I head off optimistically to search the beach. Others might decide it is not even worth their while on such a day. Once I get going, I always find something that I have not noticed before.

What are the leadership lessons here? And the family lessons?

Remember the song from The King and I *..... "Whenever I feel afraid...?"*

Does smiling habitually actually result in improved inner well-being?

Does smiling habitually and choosing the glass half-full perspective actually result in others responding with enthusiasm?

When is it necessary to do a reality check?

Plenitude Stymies Creativity

When the beach is full of intriguing shells, it is hard to draw myself away to mull and ponder. The allure of the immediate makes abstract thinking well nigh impossible.

There are two tactics possible. One, give in and enjoy the plenitude, as later walks probably will not bring such distractions. Two, if there have been too many of these short-term feeding frenzy opportunities, then I can purposely choose to walk the beach level where there are fewer treasures so that long-term thinking can occur. Or, to have your cake and eat it, too, set aside a gathering time and a separate visioning time.

Remember Anne Morrow Lindbergh's retreat to a cabin with no electricity to enable the distance and time she needed to be creative? The result was *Gift from the Sea*.

In your personal life, what kinds of plenitude negatively impact your growth?

In business settings, how does a period of high demand for one's goods or services impact long-term planning?

What strategies can you employ to ensure critical assessment and planning time?

Don't Put All of
Your Shells in One Bucket

Women are especially fortunate in that we tend to have multiple buckets going at any given time. Studies have shown that those who invest their energies (not to mention their finances) in a variety of enterprises are less vulnerable when downturns in one segment occur. Their other interests keep them buoyant (*Lifeprints: Today's Women – 1983*).

Your buckets may be as diverse as your workplace, your volunteer commitments, your family and extended family, your neighborhood, and your church.

Recognize that your dispersal of your energies, far from being indiscriminate, undisciplined, dilettantish, or whatever other negative you could use to define your pattern, may indeed be both your saving grace and may provide serendipitous connections.

I visualize one purple bucket, one yellow bucket, a green, orange, and rose...just waiting for me on the porch as I leave for my morning beach excursion.

What are some of your buckets?

Which one(s) have been empty or diminished at times?

Which one(s) have been full?

Has your life stage had anything to do with the fullness or emptiness of some of your buckets?

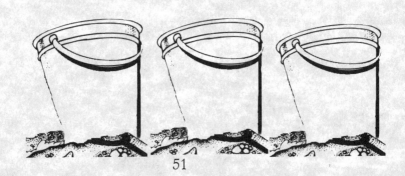

Scarcity vs. Plenty

If one has any inclination toward believing that life's provisions are limited and scarce, then Sanibel Island beach is the cure! When folks return from the "same" morning walk (that by now we know is never the same), there will be as many various assessments as there are people.

When someone says, "There's nothing out there," we need to query further and understand his needs, wishes, or requirements. If he is seeking only one hard-to-find specimen, he may not have found it today. If he is more flexible and has learned how to cope with the vagaries of the supply, he may have been able to set aside all of the Figs he will need for a whole year. While hoarding is not admirable, good resource management is.

There are those on the beach who feel a certain superiority when they see eager children or other novices collecting shells that they do not value. Delight is a rare and wonderful experience – probably more valuable than any shells being collected.

Do you basically see the glass as half-full or half-empty?

By knowing any negative predilection, can you make corrective adjustments?

Can you team up with a half-full cohort?

Belief in sufficiency tends to result in its fulfillment.

Playfulness and Prosperity

The beach promotes an attitude of curiosity and playfulness that is worthy of inclusion in the rest of our life. In the midst of the profusion of shells, the warmth of the sun, and the remarkable vistas, we feel prosperous beyond measure. People wear more colorful and creative outfits at the beach than they would ever consider "at home." But, these outward symbols of our playfulness could set the tone for a breath of fresh air in our workplace and our families.

Some years ago I found two accessories that are sure-fire conversation starters wherever I go. One is a multi-strand necklace with a Crayola-like display of colored ovals – made from re-cycled tires! I can even wear it while swimming! Cleopatra in the pool!

The other is a tie made of the same material with a band to slip around one's neck. Painted in tones of oranges, pinks, and yellows in the Jackson Pollock style, it can be worn by men or women.

When I wear these outrageous items to work or a church gathering, they put the world on notice that I'm in a fun-loving, creative mood.

How could you adapt these for your next staff meeting or annual meeting of your volunteer board? Magical ideas will flow and prosperity will not be far behind!

Look at the glorious beach towels available as pieces of art. Hang a few as tapestries on your conference room walls and watch the change in your meeting flavor.

*P.S. The Cleopatra necklace originally came with three strands. One of our staff counselors said, "Oh, my daughter would think she'd died and gone to heaven if she had a necklace like that!" That evening, I detached one strand and added a Velcro clasp. It is fun being in the "died and gone to heaven" business!

The Importance of Very Small Shells

It is very easy to get so focused on the big or flashy specimens that we forget to collect little treasures as well. This is critical for two reasons:

- *we need to fill in around the gaps created by the "stars;"*
- *we may have some smaller scale projects in which these little shells would be "stars."*

Many large corporations have made the decision (faulty, I believe) to get rid of a lot of their "tuckers," their very little shells. The end result is that they either have holes not covered by their bigger shells or must overlap them in order to gain coverage (an expensive endeavor that often causes turf battles and thoughts that they are too important to be doing what they perceive as menial tasks).

For example, one year an organization under major budget constraints did away with janitorial services and landscape maintenance. Additionally, the decision was made to amalgamate almost all of the administrative services in a building separate from most of the functions needing support. (This was prior to computer linkage that helped connect outlying departments.) Do you think that anyone could admit that his position was so unimportant that he could do a few of those tasks? Only by organizing clean up days for all hands, including the senior leaders, did the duties get done sporadically. By mid-year, the situation was so embarrassing to the corporate leaders that they re-thought their decisions.

Could some of your "tuckers" be folks who are new to the workplace and learning your business? If so, what message do we send when we think we could easily do without their functions?

How can we maximize the productivity and value of each of our members (of our family, workplace, or volunteer space)?

Fractures or Growth Lines?

On the Conchs, which grow to be giants, there are often vertical lines which appear to be either growth or fracture marks. The pattern is interrupted slightly at this point and there seems to be greater thickness as well.

It reminds me of the frequency with which particularly active children experience broken bones – and not just children! The line also reminds me of the so-called "growing pains" that can occur when folks are growing faster than the rest of their bodies can accommodate. I think this also happens in professional growth for individuals and groups. A fracture can mend stronger than the original and growth leaves scars as well.

As leaders or parents, we may tend to want to protect individuals or groups from what seems at first glance to be damage. But, perhaps more damaging would be risk avoidance and smothering – the path to barnacles!

As we select and retain folks with fracture or growth lines, perhaps the wisest approach would be to assess with them what they see as the impact and what strengths and weaknesses have resulted. This is a real leadership opportunity.

Have you personally experienced any fractures or growth lines (including those infamous stretch marks)? If so, what strengths and weaknesses have you assessed as a result?

Has your family experienced the above? The results?

Has your workplace or volunteer arena (such as your church) experienced the above? The results?

Barnacles

I choose some Scallop shells with one or two Barnacles. They give the Scallops the appearance of a soft lavender lacy bonnet. However, I limit the number used in any one project.

Barnacles usually attach themselves to stationary objects (animate and inanimate). Mobile creatures are like rolling stones – they gather no moss (or Barnacles). If a Barnacle has not been attached very long, you often can remove it easily.

Most boat owners paint their underwater surfaces with an anti-fouling paint in order to deter Barnacle build up. While Barnacles don't actually destroy the boat like the Teredo Worms do, their accumulation does slow down the boat's passage through the water.

Likewise, organizations would be wise to treat their submerged stationary members to a protective covering and they could rotate those with this duty to allow periodic scraping and cleaning.

How does this concept apply to your life?

How does this concept apply to your workplace?

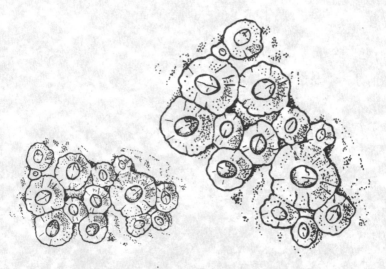

Barnacle Remover

As we are all likely to get Barnacles at one time or another, even on our most prized products, it is really important to have a Barnacle Remover.

This is either a person or a process. A spouse, co-worker, or really good friend can serve as the one to notice and help to eliminate the unattractive growth.

In some situations, a process may help us identify blemishes and rectify our performance.

On a personal level, who or what performs this duty for you? A spouse, friend, co-worker, women's network, or an academic or spiritual connection?

On a professional level, are there benchmarks, quarterly reviews and reports, quality review boards, etc?

It would be optimum to recognize a Barnacle in the early stages. What are the warning signs?

*P. S. My Barnacle Remover husband also sands the rough edges on some of my prize shells! Who sands your edges?

Museum Displays

Sometimes a life-cycle display of the same shell can be very enlightening. Seeing its size and shape as it develops into its mature version can help us identify immature specimens more readily.

As a scientific progression, this arrangement can be illuminating. However, in a workplace one would rarely encounter such singularity of type – unless it is a family business or one determined to have all employees fit the same mold. Perhaps we encounter this phenomenon in some highly structured families, in primary school settings, religious denominations that insist on adherence to articulated dogma, and in circumstances where "wanna be's" twist themselves to copy someone powerful.

Does this concept apply to your life?

Does this concept apply to your workplace?

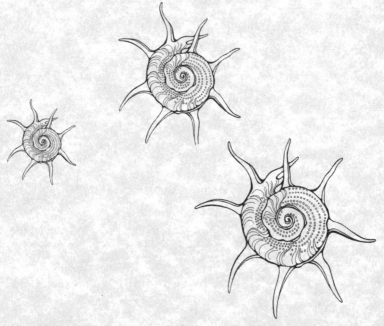

Rewards and Recognition

When your group represents a pocket of excellence, a one-size-fits-all system of awards is inappropriate. In the workplace or volunteer setting, remarkable individuals act as both magnets and catalysts. Others want to be part of a team with them, believing that they are measured and motivated by the company they keep.

If the corporate policy and budget is not flexible, then a strategic leader needs to work with the group to find alternative ways that are meaningful to the group and to given individuals.

Just as you would not compare a Lace Murex to a Fighting Conch on the beach, you need to recognize those who are stellar in a variety of ways.

Send one to a special training or conference she has desired.

Write a press release on the activities of one of your innovative individuals or teams and send it to the local newspaper and professional or collegiate journals that would showcase their work to neighbors and peers.

Arrange a ceremony with senior management taking note of an accomplishment.

Enter your stars in corporate or professional competitions.

Ensure that annual performance reviews are timely testimonials to achievements and request input for the final write-up from the individuals themselves. The purpose is two-fold: it helps with self-appraisal awareness (which is not a skill that comes easily to everyone), and it provides training for the time when they have supervisory responsibilities. Learning how to accurately evaluate one's own work and that of others, and then translate that to a written (and oral) performance rating happens best in a safe and nurturing environment.

External measurement of your group's success is also valuable.

Many industries have benchmarking procedures, product testing, and accreditation processes. If, for example, your high school faculty consistently produces students with perfect 800's on their SAT exams or produces a number of state teachers of the year, then you have a pocket of excellence. If your teams consistently produce Olympic competitors or the best safety record in your business, they are exceptional.

Immediate personal attention when someone has done something "just right" is the easiest and, in some ways, the best recognition. It happens frequently in the best groups and praise can come from the boss, one's peers, or one's "reports." "Well done, Dad!" is to be cherished.

Quite remarkably, in an environment that celebrates the small stuff, folks begin to notice their own "just rights" and their endorphins flow.

While this may sound pretty basic, the truth is that many workplaces, volunteer settings, and families fail at the critical point of recognition, often due to some inappropriate sensitivity as to how those not winning the awards this time may feel. Certainly, awards should be delivered in a professional way; but, the bottom line is that you want to keep your stars performing and hope to nudge others to make their best effort.

The group usually knows the lay of the land and there will be few surprises. Even school children are keen observers and know who is good at what.

For insights, visit other beaches – especially world-class beaches!

Participate on teams to accredit or assess your peers.
Learn what they do well (so you can mimic),
and learn from what they do poorly so that
you can avoid those practices.

Happy Shells

There are shells that make you smile just to see them on the beach – whether you pick them up for your collection or not.

The Buttercup Lucina with its jaunty yellow-gold rim inside fairly shouts joy, especially when it is damp with dew or sea spray.

The yellow, orange, and silver Jingles, almost transparent, sparkle with their natural sheen. The Yellow Cockle is an irrepressible optimist, as sunny on the inside as the outside. His relative, the Egg Cockle, has a natural Teflon – nothing sticks to the surface.

And, the Sunrise Tellins, often found as a light yellow pair, surprise you with their luminescent interiors.

Having a few of these ever-cheerful shells in your collection ensures that even when events and experiences are gloomy, there is a reminder of delight. Decorators tell us how important it is to have some yellow in each room – especially in an office.

Do you know people who are your happy shells?

How do they impact your life?

How do they impact a workplace?

I read in the program notes for a recent performance of Johannes Brahms' "A German Requiem," that he left a dinner party because it was "too exasperating to have the lady on his right talking in E major and the lady on his left talking in E minor!" While the reviewer attributed his discomfort to his sensitive ears, I wonder if it was more a philosophical sensitivity.

Drills Make Holes

Almost all Clamshells, Mussels, or other Mollusks on the beach have a hole in them. That is usually the reason they are there. They have been drilled by an Auger or a Cerith, or by their larger pal predators, the Turritella and the Moon Snail. A drill sucks the life out of its prey.

Life is like that for human beings, too. There often has been an experience that drives folks to look for new workplaces, churches, or social groups. For them, their "hole" feels very large and visible.

However, the truth is that the human versions rarely have been permanently impaired by their skewering. With wise positioning, they can perform from their strengths and fairest angles. Able leaders will enable them to patch their holes and get on with what they do best.

Do you know people who are drills?

Do you know people who have been drilled?

How do they impact your life?

How do they impact a workplace?

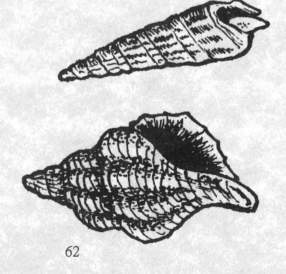

Day of Figs (not to be confused with the Bay of Pigs!)

Fig shells usually are not numerous during my Sanibel Island visits. However, climatic conditions have given me two opportunities over the last decade to collect a number of these gracefully curved beauties ranging in hue from light beige to tobacco. Their delicate ribbing gives texture and strength to their thin skins. When nature presents me with this rare opportunity, I gleefully collect them and carry them gingerly. I use a few immediately and store others for future projects.

Similar circumstances occur in social settings and workplaces.

Some years ago, my corporate comptroller called and said he had the rare combination of funds and billets if I could hire up to nine specialists quickly. He knew that we had a long waiting list for one of our labor-intensive services and thought this would aid families enormously.

Working with our personnel department, with whom we had an unusually good rapport, we were able to recruit nine specialists who met very demanding credentials, but who also had talents that could eventually help them move throughout our organization as openings permitted.

Being ready to take advantage of a windfall is a key leadership skill. By choice you are ready; by chance opportunity appears. Others will call you "lucky." In some ways, that demeans your foresight, preparation, and collaborative networking that were intentional ingredients of your success.

How has this concept played out in your personal life?

How has this concept played out in your professional life?

What preparations can you make in intellectual, material, and process realms that would enable you to benefit from a windfall?

Surfeit

When we really are in tune with the natural rhythms of the beach (and ourselves), we sense when enough is enough – enough shell collecting, shopping, eating, and working. Even the little scurry birds rest periodically and take time for personal maintenance.

Pace is part of the issue. The other part is consumption (of things, time, energy, and emotions). Each of us has our own metabolism and menu, so we need to find our own best balance.

When we are off-balance, we send that message subliminally to the world around us. We will be diminished in some eyes (including our own) by our lack of control.

Have you ever felt uncomfortably full (or thought your closet looked this way)? What precipitated this? Do you know some solutions (and preventions)?

Have you felt overwhelmed at work? How did it occur? What were the outcomes?

Can you control the prevention and solutions yourself?

Do you need others to collaborate to effect your own changes?

Look Behind You

As my husband and I entered the "Ding" Darling Nature Preserve on Easter Sunday morning, the tide was already very far out – usually a good sign for concentrated feeding areas for the birds. We were immediately drawn to the water on the left of the road where an amazing variety were feeding. One other viewer was there and others joined.

As we started to return to our car, my husband said, "Look behind you!" There, in the mix of shadows and sun, was a large flock of Roseate Spoonbills – the favorite bird of many visitors. Most had finished feeding, so were preening and stretching out their wings. The sun cast this choreography in reflections on the water and doubled their amazing performance. Before long, they folded their circus candy bodies into the nearby trees for their morning nap.

We are often so focused on one issue or experience that we fail to notice other sources of delight.

Can you think of instances when this has been true for you?

What might you have missed?

When a fellow visitor at the next site was exclaiming over one Roseate Spoonbill and was elated by the arrival of a second, I kept quiet about what he had missed at the prior stop. No doubt, we have all missed remarkable experiences.......

Look Above You

At Sanibel Island, a clear evening brings an exciting sky. The North Star, Venus, Mars, Orion's Belt, and the Big Dipper are all visible in this Northern Hemisphere sky. In fact, these are our staples wherever we live and travel in this hemisphere.

What a comfort to be able to see these "landmarks" in our evening and sometimes early morning skies. When I walk my Black Labrador in Connecticut, we see many of these same constellations at early dawn. "God's in His heaven – all's right with the world" (Robert Browning).

Metaphorically, what is above you? Can you see it clearly or is it obstructed by cloud cover?

What are the usual constellations there?

A comet brings excitement. What is the equivalent for you personally? Professionally?

Look a Gift Shell in the Mouth

Try to avoid being given shells from someone else's collection. They obviously weren't special enough to keep and the human versions sense that.

Pass-alongs usually end up being passed along yet again, but sometimes only after they have occupied precious space and perhaps have deprived you of time and energy for their maintenance. When corporate realignments cause the merging of a malfunctioning unit into a highly productive setting, rough seas and stormy weather are ahead!

The pass-alongs know the score and they suspect that they will have even less freedom from supervision in the new amalgam, so they are literally dragged kicking, screaming, and filing EEO complaints. It takes a strong leader to acculturate those who are willing to try, and to separate those unwilling or incapable of fulfilling their tasks. Some will resort to subterfuge while appearing to accommodate.

These are the "gifts from hell" – not gifts from the sea!

What has been your experience with pass-alongs in your personal life?

What has been your experience with pass-alongs in your workplace?

What policies and regulations require pass-alongs and enable them to make the transition difficult?

What strategies have you found that ameliorate the phenomenon?

Sea Grapes

One of the favorite plantings at Sanibel is the Sea Grape, a woody shrub/tree that has wonderful large saucer-like leathery leaves and assumes asymmetrical shapes. The newest leaves are shiny and light green. Older leaves are dark green, and mature leaves are red. So, when breezes blow, they dance in colorful profusion.

Most are trimmed in an attempt to control their shape and size. The result is that few ever are able to offer their blossoms (both yellow and red on the same tree!) and, therefore, no grapes appear. It was only on a wild beach in the Caribbean that I encountered the gorgeous clumps of grapes.

In our attempts to cut this specimen into an artificial shape or stature, we eliminate its blossoms and fruit. Is there a human counterpart to this story?

We should not plant ourselves or others willy-nilly. What environment do you know is best for your flowers and fruit?

What repositioning or replanting should you do in your workplace in order to enable flowering and fruit?

As you select new plants (employees), what can the Sea Grapes teach you?

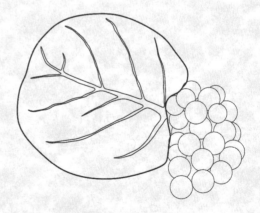

Sponges

When I come upon Sponges freshly deposited by the tide, I am astounded by their Saguaro-like shapes and their brilliant colors: orange, red, bright yellow, and purple. When they remain in their marine environment, they stand tall on their stalk. But, storms uproot them and they have no ability to re-attach. They must float where the waves take them and then litter the beach, turning brown in the sun.

Drawn to their color on the beach, I often long to collect them for some exotic "floral" arrangement. But, I have learned from experience that it is impossible to get the smell out of them. Every time the humidity increases, their odor factor escalates and they are an embarrassment waiting to happen.

Human Sponges can be beautiful, if left undisturbed in situ. They serve as filters of microscopic organisms and enable fish and other small critters a camouflaging environment.

Managers take note: if your Sponges are serving a positive environmental purpose and not harming their host(s), leave them in place. Be aware that they are not able to tolerate disruption. Their contribution is small; but, if you can afford them, they are beautiful filters for your workplace.

Have you encountered love sponges? Attention sponges? Crisis sponges?

What mistakes did you make in regard to them?

What did you learn?

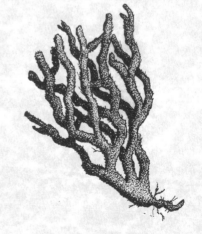

Everyone Needs a Good Operculum!

Every univalve (Snail, Conch, Whelk, etc.) has an operculum. It is the hard "door" that he closes when his long soft (vulnerable) "foot" is inside his shell. It is his primary protection from predators.

Many of us have been socialized to be open and accommodating, so we find the concept of a gate and a gatekeeper not only foreign, but rather offensive. However, if we cannot perform the function for ourselves, we need to find someone who will.

In order to protect our time, energy, focus, and resources, we do need a gate, albeit visibly open while functionally impenetrable. Like the decorative ironwork grilles found in many warm climates, it performs the duty of a checkpoint.

In a democratic society and in customer-focused businesses, we can become laissez-faire to our own detriment. We need to know how to say "No," and close the door.

How would an operculum be useful in your personal relationships?

What function would an operculum serve in your professional life?

What vulnerabilities would an operculum protect for you?

Extreme High and Low Tides

The Gulf Coast, unlike the Atlantic Coast, has some aberrant tides. There will be several days in a row when instead of two sets of tides, there will be only one, widely separated and with extreme highs or lows.

Are they windows of opportunity?

How do the wildlife sense these changes? (i.e., how did elephants and native tribes anticipate the Asian tsunami?)

Could our low tide be the equivalent of getting our inventory down or really weeding out unused items?

What would be the equivalent of an exceedingly high tide?

Are there risks? Benefits?

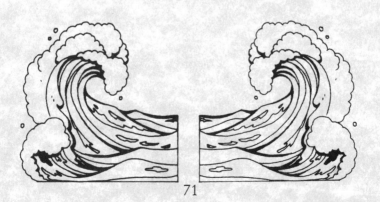

Beach Protocol

Amy Vanderbilt could have written this! The rules are the same at the beach as they are at the dinner table or shopping in a fancy store.

Don't cut in line. Those who run up and cut in front of you and slow down are just as obnoxious on the sand as on the highway.

Don't walk just off the shoulder of someone ahead of you. You intrude upon his search and his reverie. A woman may find this feels like stalking. Either speed up or fall back a bit.

Don't walk between a mother and her child at the water's edge. And, don't walk between a fisherman's pole and the water, even if the pole is untended and in a stand. The line can be invisible and his rage won't be!

If you are jogging through, don't run right where all of the newest shells are!

If you pick it up, put it back gently. If it was worth looking at intently, it is worth replacing without damage. (This is particularly applicable in the recruiting process for those you choose not to select.)

Take only what you can use. Make sure your non-selectees are back out on the beach promptly and without compromise.

Don't be greedy. Those chosen by greedy collectors worry whether they will make the cut later and may not commit to the enterprise. They feel a certain one-upsmanship in leaving for another operation in which they will be more cherished.

Don't presume to tell fellow collectors what they will find. That is controlling and presumes they are looking for the same items. They may be looking for something quite different and may find something you missed or were not looking for.

Take all of your trash with you and even that of others. The Girl Scout in me picks up the shards of glass, the relics of aluminum cans waiting to carve up someone's foot, the plastic bags, and personal items left or washed up on the beach. At Sanibel Island, this debris is remarkably rare, both because people consciously avoid littering and consciously collect trash. The beauty of the environment seems to bring out the best in most.

In our corporate environments, we should be as conscientious about our debris (emotional and physical). There is no excuse for messy offices, waiting rooms, staff lounges, and spaces outside of our buildings. They all reflect a lack of caring and responsibility that our customers notice and calibrate.

What trash remains uncollected in your front yard (residential or corporate)?

How can etiquette/protocol enhance your relationships with family? With customers?

If you were to design/delineate the etiquette for your family, workplace, or volunteer arena, what elements would it include?

How could you disseminate this?

How could you ensure its enculturation? (i.e., could its observance become part of the requirements for promotion?).

An Osprey's Call

The "I'm coming home" call from an Osprey is unmistakable. He or she is headed home with a fish or nesting material. Neither assumes to arrive unannounced.

When a great bird is flying overhead and I'm trying to identify him quickly, I am struck by the fact that the Osprey is so precise about announcing arrival. He or she doesn't need a cell phone! Both check in with the other before arriving at the nest, so neither is worried about a predator. It may also be an announcement of success. What a gracious and connected relationship they have.

In our own fast-paced world, how do we notify those most important to us about our activities and schedule?

High-tech:

Low-tech:

How do we ensure that our motivation is to apprise and not control?

Leave
Your Cell Phone
at Home!

Don't walk the beach with your cell phone in use! In spite of the fact that you believe you can be in two modes at once, the truth is that you can't. You may be able to achieve the superficial level of geographically arriving at your dream vacation destination, but the minute you check in with the office, you are somewhere else.

You need to be here – away from all of the other pieces of your life. You need to experience life **Now – Here** – and, if you're lucky, **Why?** You need to step out of your mainstream into an experience that will magnify your time, insight, and sensitivity – all of these immeasurables and unquantifiables. Dare to disconnect and be rewarded.

When you use your cell phone while on vacation, what is your motivation?

Do you fear that the office will get along without you?

Have you enough trust in your cohorts to allow them both responsibility and authority to make decisions without you?

Wouldn't you be doing yourself and your office a favor to get truly rested and renewed?

Can the same be true for your extended family? Let one gatekeeper know your destination and contact information and make the judgment call on whether to disrupt you on vacation or not.

A wonderful cartoon shows a mermaid holding a conch shell to her ear.

In Reverence
is the Preservation
of Serenity

A la Thoreau's "In wildness is the preservation of the world," we need quiet to balance the noise of all sorts around us. When a space is silent, one is challenged to listen even more intently than usual to decipher the whispers of sound encountered.

Along a dike in Tarpon Bay early in the morning, one is brushed by spider webs across the mangrove branches – sure indication that no one else has entered these gossamer portals before us. The only sounds audible are the calls of a pair of Cardinals, the skittering of small lizards among the dry palm fronds, and the sound of Sea Grape leaves falling.

I am saddened as a raucous family of four, banging their paddles against their canoes, not only disturb my quiet reverie and chase away all wildlife within their range, but they will miss the experience of reverence in a wild sanctuary. Their lives will be diminished because they have not learned. It is more than manners. It is sensitivity to and a respect for their environment – both natural and human.

Do you have favorite places that bring serenity? Physical places? Mental places?

How can you model reverence for solitude? In your family? In your workplace?

What losses occur when solitude is not frequent?

Not Seeing the Forest

On the beach at sunrise there is artistry rarely seen or noticed by passersby. The receding tide leaves a series of gossamer strands and textured shadings to mark its retreat. Seen from the shoreline, it resembles a series of mountains etched on sand-colored glass or shrouded in a beige mist. Each wave leaves a slightly different collection of miniscule particles, so each thread outlines a slightly different texture illuminated by the early sun.

One must consciously focus on this evanescent scenery instead of the shell shapes in order to see its beauty. So, too, in life, in the stillness of dawn, before the day brings footprints across this precious landscape, we should pause and search the lifescape before us.

In the workplace, an application would be to honor folks' quiet time when they come in before "shop opens up." Allow them the untrampled beach view without interruption. They will be likely to have a far more productive day than if they immediately have fires to put out.

What is your forest and what are your trees?

What other strategies could help you see the forest vs. the trees?

Ink Fish

Very rarely at Sanibel Island we see a creature called an Ink Fish. He really is a Sea Slug with thin membrane-like "wings" that fold around his body and allow him to fly in the water. So, when he is in his environment, he has quite an effective locomotion... especially for a Slug.

However, when he is beached, he is at the mercy of the environment. He needs water to refloat. If he is threatened, he squirts a reddish purple "ink."

How like his human counterparts who whip out their red pens!

Do you know any Ink Fish?

What color of ink do you use for yourself and others when you edit or make written comments? Psychologically, any color other than red would be preferable!

Mix and Match

We have all heard talks on how to select our travel clothes and how to pack them without wrinkles. The concepts of color coordination, layering, and multiple combinations abound.

What we often fail to factor into our packing list are the items and uses that are more mundane. We remember the Captain's Dinner or resort attire, but we forget that we sometimes get very cold at night or in air-conditioned spaces. Do we have enough wraps and wind jackets to repel cool damp evenings? Fancy shoes are on the list, but do we have tried and true tennis shoes and socks to prevent blisters, or at least hide the bandages, from too much walking?

How do we balance the glamorous, the daily, and the emergency apparel/ gear? Of course, the destination will determine the availability of some of these items.

In your personal baggage, how much space do you allot to the arenas of glamour, mundane, and emergency?

Is this the same proportion you find in your business or volunteer settings?

Do you plan your packing methodically or do you wait 'til the last minute?

Some folks find that anticipation is a major ingredient in their enjoyment of the whole trip, as is their re-living of the event through photos and journals. What is your philosophy?

DANGERS...

Eroding the Beach

When I see a "Shell Shark" digging away at drop-offs caused by high waves, I think how vulnerable to erosion she is making a fragile shoreline. All in the name of finding special shells, she gouges the bank.

Interested only in short-term gain, she seems to care nothing for the long-term impact. Although the beach belongs to the public up to the historic high water line, adjacent property owners must feel very threatened by such activity, literally watching their front yards shrink.

The corporate equivalent could be the bean-counter who decides to cut a certain percentage from the budget, no matter what the long-term impact. She searches the landscape for easy raids.

What or who is nibbling away at your shoreline?

Why?

What can you do about it?

Bandages

There are lots of bandages on the beach today. Maybe I am more keenly aware because I am wearing a few myself – the results of walking too far and too fast these last few days when the unusual tides brought rare opportunities.

Keeping the bandages on is practically impossible once my feet are wet, whether in my beach shoes or barefoot. What to do? There must be a lot of "walking wounded" like me.

Should I toughen up my feet, getting calluses by walking in the "shell hash" — the tiny little shells that glisten like glass particles as the waves retreat.

Should I choose higher ground that is less strewn with shells?

Should I carry a lot of bandages?

How does this metaphor apply personally and professionally?

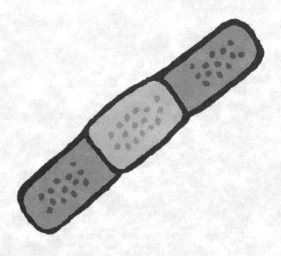

84

Fear

One afternoon as I was walking alone on the beach, quite far away from our cabin and any other people, I saw a woman in what looked like distress. As I scurried along in her direction, I saw her standing frozen about eight feet from shore. When I asked if I could help, she pointed to the water in front of her.

I had been so focused on her that I had failed to see the huge migration of Stingrays that was headed west, as many as three wide and almost touching those in front of them. No wonder she was standing still as they paraded past her.

It felt like ages that I stood there, being human company, but not any physical help. Though I offered my hand, she was fearful of stepping into the middle of the ominous dark shapes as they passed by at warp speed. Finally, finally ... they were gone and she was grateful for my assist ashore.

When I described this terrifying experience to my husband, he chuckled and said that at any point she or I could have walked into the midst of the Stingrays and they would simply have swum around us! He said that the only time that a Stingray is potentially dangerous is if he has covered himself in the sand near the shore and a swimmer steps on him – so it is wise to shuffle into the water. That information would have empowered me!

On any given day, when all else seems quite normal, your life can be interrupted by a string of Stingrays. What is important to remember is that you need to ask for help and you need to be aware that in spite of their perceived volume and venom, they would move around you harmlessly if you have the courage to venture across. Clearly, we need to know our own courage factor and it would be very helpful to know the capability and intent of our invaders.

Are they dangerous?

Do they mean damage?

Are they simply passing through?

What precautions would I take in the future?

What experiences have you had where information would have diminished fear?

What episodes in your workplace remind you of this scenario?

What experiences have you had where information would have diminished fear?

Yes, Virginia,
There are Alligators:
A Cautionary Tale

Even in paradise, there are creatures that can harm you. On Sanibel Island, in the Gulf of Mexico, there is a wonderful opportunity to observe and learn to identify a wide range of birds, animals, and other wildlife. But, the big attraction for children is to see an Alligator. It is both exciting and fearsome at the same time.

As you begin to be aware of an Alligator's size, speed, and seemingly sleepy pose, Virginia, you should watch his eyes and know that he is hearing everything. He is often wily, positioning himself on a bank where he has a view of the pond, but is screened by a small bush. When the raucous Moorhen comes to the bank, announcing her approach for all to hear and sporting her flashy orange-red beak, she peers at the grass before walking up the rise. Unfortunately, because of the incline and the small bush, the Moorhen does not see what awaits her. She is in search of food and really isn't expecting to be the Alligator's lunch. But...

In order not to become an Alligator's lunch, Virginia, you should learn the sort of low croaking or grunting sound that an Alligator makes. That way, when marsh grasses screen a small pond or riverbank, you can be alert to his sound. You should also be wary when you see what look like paths leading through cattails and tall grasses to a waterway. Those will be his favorite routes.

When walking in wild places, always go with at least one other person. Stick to the well-traveled walkways, and don't go too close to the edge of any bodies of water. If you see an Alligator, turn and go another way... and keep a careful eye out behind you.

An Alligator is much like other sources of danger in your life, Virginia. It is natural to feel a little curious about risky behaviors and potentially harmful people. But, knowing about their characteristics and how to avoid them gives you the advantage. Not all harmful behaviors and people are as clearly identifiable as an Alligator. That is the challenge for your lifetime, Virginia. But, don't get so focused on avoiding Alligators that you fail to enjoy the journey.

What are some of your Alligators?

What are their favorite hiding places?

What guises or camouflage do they use?

Would they like you for lunch?

Running
the Gauntlet

Yesterday, my husband and I were the first visitors to the Bailey Tract (a small section of the "Ding" Darling Nature Preserve that is closer to the resort and residential areas). As we walked down the path to the map kiosk, we heard loud grunts to the left and the right of us – several on each side! Trying to allay my fears, my husband said, "Bullfrogs." I knew they were an antiphonal choir of Alligators announcing the first visitors of the morning. With the pond waters especially high due to recent rains, I was not a happy camper.

We have walked that area many times before and have rarely felt the presence of one or two Alligators – much less double that and quadruple the vocalizations this time.

It was hard to focus on seeing anything else while we walked the tract. Along the extra high water canal where we have seen Alligators before, I looked around and behind me often. As we got ready to leave, I found my worries escalating, even though we had seen numerous other visitors in the interim.

Not a comment as we left! Not a single grunt. Was this the Alligators' early alert, "Here they come!" communication? It certainly sounded ominous to me.

While this was not the Navy Tailhook scenario, do the first folks down a given path hear threats and taunts?

How do we handle this phenomenon?

Should there be signs warning visitors? Would some be scared off? Would some be attracted?

Do those who come later have any sense that forerunners blazed the trail?

Shark Alert!

On a recent two-week vacation at Sanibel Island, we were distressed to learn in the first few days of a Shark attack in front of the inn next door. Emergency paramedics had responded. It happened shortly after we had returned from our morning shell walk, and we thought we could picture the victim. We had seen him putting on his chartreuse flippers and his chartreuse and black goggles.

In our decade-plus of visits, we have never been aware of Sharks in the water. But, this year, after the distressing news, a Shark appeared daily almost on schedule about four o'clock. Many people on the beach saw him and yet, no mention in local newspapers or flyers to hotel visitors.

More than a week later, a blue flyer was tacked to a palm tree at the entrance of the public access I use daily in the afternoon. It was an alert (giving a date five days after the original incident we knew about). It also listed precautions such as not wearing metallic trim on your bathing suit, avoiding areas where high bird feeding would indicate schooling fish, and avoiding the run off sloughs created by sandbars.

Good advice, but not much publicity. I suspect the same holds true about Shark sightings and attacks in workplaces. In a misguided attempt to sanitize the corporate reputation, the powers-that-be avoid public comment. So, word of mouth must be the primary communication tool. That becomes iffy, as veracity can be doubted. Also, there is the element of not wanting to worry unduly the innocents playing in the water. The big question is, what is "unduly?"

90

One of the commonly held beliefs is that Sharks are not found where there are Dolphins (or Porpoises). Not true, said the blue flyer on the palm tree. So, the presence of remarkable large beneficent creatures does not preclude a Shark's presence. Note that a Shark is often found in the midst of a feeding frenzy, where he can operate in the midst of chaos almost undetected.

Doesn't this sound a lot like some workplaces?

Who are some Sharks you know?

What scenarios are their favorite milieux?

How do you know of their presence?

Sunburn,
Sharp Shells,
and "No-seeums"

Safety is a concern even in paradise. Folks are generally aware of the need for dark glasses (even for children) and suntan lotion with a high block number.

Prevention is the name of the game for dehydration, cut feet, and the invisible swarm of sand gnats when the breeze stops or the temperature is at its most delightful. Most beachcombers sport mesh shoes, because even swimming can be treacherous if you stand up in the water. "Skin-so-soft" is the scent of choice for repelling the sand gnats; perfume and hair sprays have the opposite effect.

Every environment has its challenges, even dangers.
What are yours?

What precautions do you take for prevention?

What is in your first aid kit?

And now, the trick question: are you allowed by corporate rules to share the contents of your first aid kit? In this litigious society, you may be required to suggest that your bandage-requesting co-worker see the staff or school nurse or visit the employee assistance program provider.

I carry bandages in my beach bag for myself and others.

Camelot

One of the most remarkable qualities of Sanibel is its almost Camelot-like quality (in spite of the enormous growth of condos and visitors). The beach is almost trash-free – when I carry my net bag for shells that is big enough to stash debris plus treasures, I hardly ever have to pick up the sorts of things you find dropped or washed ashore elsewhere. Those who visit seem to sense how very special it is and do their part to keep it that way.

People usually avoid walking on the shells, choosing higher or lower ground, depending on the tide. If they are not shelling, they move around shell banks and other people, just like the birds. They do not intrude upon someone else's space – be that shell space or reverie. When appropriate eye contact occurs, there may be pleasant greetings or a question about some specimen they have found and don't recognize. Mostly, the noise of the waves serves as an audial cocoon.

None of the birds seems phased by humans, which shows that people have behaved very well in their interface both at the preserves and beaches.

What leadership lessons can be taken from this Camelot?

Trust and Freedom

It amazes me that even on the most heavily used public beaches at Sanibel Island, people set down their gear and then go off to shell or walk some distance. They have trust that their belongings will be untouched and that gives them freedom to explore.

Can you do the equivalent in your workplace or do you lock your office? When we have to be concerned about theft of an item or an idea, we are less likely to put it on the beach.

In some settings, the office supplies are locked up; not so in others. In one setting, employees actually put their name on the underside of portable equipment and furniture because fellow workers came in over the weekend (a "no-no" all by itself) and relocated items to their own offices. When caught because of an owner's name, they weren't at all embarrassed or apologetic. "I needed it," was the Goldilocks-style explanation.

When even just one person abrogates the trust environment, everyone feels at risk. The same is true with ideas.

Have you ever experienced theft of items or ideas?

How did it feel?

How can you positively impact your environment for trust?

In the domain of ideas, it is critical to credit the originator. Failure to do so will cost you ideas and, in all likelihood, that innovative employee who will move on. We are not even talking about copyright and patent level material here, which obviously enters a much-regulated level.

How can you document your ideas as a precaution against theft or the more subtle non-recognition strategy (which results in your idea emerging from someone else's mouth a week later)?

The Impact of Storms

Although the turbulence may be well out to sea, the results eventually appear on our beach in the form of eroding waves, murky waters, traps washed ashore, and the dislocation of many species that are then tossed willy-nilly on the sand.

In a human setting, whether the external storm is financial (most turbulence has this as a key component), philosophical, or personal relations-focused, your group will be affected by its fallout.

The macro becomes micro eventually. That is why a strategic leader keeps one eye on the global or national weather and keeps the other on the home front.

What preparations and precautions can you take in advance?

Should the larger group be part of the alert, assessment, and decision-making?

Will you risk sounding like Henny Penny (of "the sky is falling" fame) or will you build a brick home (like the third little pig)?

Does taking the drill seriously help you discover pitfalls or holes that could damage your survival in the future?

Does your group appreciate your concern for their well-being?

Would they prefer less reality (as you perceive it)?

Weathering an external storm is one of the greatest challenges for leaders, second only to weathering internal storms. The strain of coping with one makes an individual, family, or group more vulnerable to the second.

Your beach will be different after the storm(s). You must salvage what is worth keeping, clean up the debris, and begin again, both humbled by the experience and determined to prevail.

Chinese Symbol
for Crisis

When our beloved islands of Sanibel and Captiva were devastated by Hurricane Charley, we heard from afar that the ubiquitous Australian Pines that lined major roads and beaches had been destroyed – leaving bare all that had been protected or camouflaged. What would the town fathers do?

Wisely, they have chosen to replant with native species (vs. the invasive non-native pines). They will use such trees as the Gumbo-Limbo and Sable Palmettos. The trees will need time to root and flourish, but long-term they will be much hardier than the faster growing species.

So, too, when our workplaces are assailed by external forces (be they economic or other storms), we need to learn the islands' lessons:

take care of the human toll – the sense of loss, lack of control, and a tendency to give up; look carefully at what structures and plantings withstood the onslaught with only minor damage; and remove the debris quickly to enable an assessment of what's next.

As the two-part Chinese symbol for crisis so clearly demonstrates, there is both destruction and opportunity in the situation. The workplace with a clear focus will be able to establish good communications (within the islands and with the world beyond). It will rally the clean up crew and the reconstruction teams and it will "do the right job right" – taking the time to select designs, materials, and plantings that will not only survive, but thrive, in the challenging environment.

What storms have you personally weathered?
What storms has your organization weathered?
What lessons did adversity bring?
What deadwood/debris was removed?
What new growth occurred as a result?

危機

Post-Hurricane Exuberance

About seven months after Hurricane Charley, I returned to find evidence of major foliage eradication, but also major growth. In fact, some species were showing double to triple the usual growth and much of it was along their trunks and big limbs because they had lost most of their secondary limbs. The clumps of greenery gave them a different profile from usual and promised significant re-forestation.

The key is that the new profile (or norm) will be different from the previous shape. Those particular trees have been changed for their lifetime.

How does this metaphor apply to your personal life?

How could it reflect a workplace that experienced a serious threat?

Does understanding that a new profile will emerge help us accept the change instead of grieving our loss?

World-Class Beach

If I'm going to shell (work), I want to be in a superb setting. Life is too short to work in mediocre environments! The resources and people that we encounter on a daily basis should simulate us to excel. The phenomenon of "ever-rising expectations" is both a challenge and an opportunity as we begin to measure our own output at this level.

My rule of thumb for assessing value is: *If it stands out on this beach...* When we work in a remarkable environment, we can be sure that something is extraordinary if it catches our attention in this rarefied arena. This is true not only of products, but of those who produce them. So, at performance evaluation time, we need to fight for the right to recognize our "stars" even when they exceed the numerical quota defined by the head office. It is a battle well worth fighting. Our "stars" need to know that they are valued.

What are some of your world-class beaches?

Who or what are some of your "stars?"

What are some creative ways to recognize or award your "stars?"

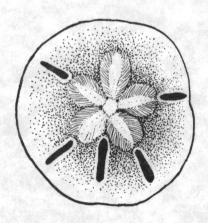

The Dangers Inherent in Being A World-Class Beach

When your workplace gets the reputation of being an exceptional place to be, you may be inundated by visitors and applicants. How does this change your setting? While gratifying, the time, energy, and space it takes to welcome these folks graciously draws resources away from your primary task, unless you can spin off a visitors' bureau to accommodate them and find ways in which they can be good business for you.

Another less positive result may occur with your stellar reputation. If your group earns a near-perfect score on its in-depth accreditation by the headquarters team, you all should celebrate! Everyone's annual evaluation should carry notice of this Q2 quotient (quality and quantity). But, be forewarned that although you are not bragging about it to your cohorts elsewhere in the system, they will take notice and there may be interesting forms of backlash as members of your team travel hither and yon.

The Snow White-style backlash may be especially noteworthy the next time the headquarters accreditation group arrives (usually with new members). They may have chips on their shoulders that are approaching redwood size and really have little or nothing to do with your team's quality. Leadership skills are indeed called for as they attempt to damage your reputation locally and nationally. Sometimes, internal malcontents who were buoyed by the success in the past seize the outgoing tide as a chance to leverage power.

The key is to seek accurate knowledge of the situation, diffuse false analyses where appropriate, and fix flaws where they do in truth exist – even if they are news to you. Blame is not in your vocabulary. You are, after all, a world-class act.

Have you experienced backlash in your personal or professional life?

Did you think that the backlash was due to your deficiencies? Look carefully to see if envy in the eyes of the beholder may be the root cause.

With this changed perspective, what strategies can you use to counter the backlash?

CORPORATE HUM:

KEEPING THE LESSONS ALIVE...

Corporate Hum

The goal of our efforts in our personal and professional lives is to reach what I call our "corporate hum." This is the level on which everything moves along with delight and productivity. It can be an ongoing or frequent experience, not just a momentary, fleeting accomplishment. You will know it when it occurs (as will those who work with you). It has the quality of an "aha" and you find yourself grinning inside and out. It is similar to the overtone that musicians know when all singers or instrumentalists are in tune. It is exhilarating. It makes all of your work worthwhile.

However, in spite of all of your careful selection, conditioning, and positioning of your shells or people, there will be a few that are not harmonious. Sometimes this lack of harmony with the whole plan is unconscious; other times, it is quite purposeful. Just like a good choral director, you need to remove those who cannot or are not singing from the same sheet of music, listening to those around them to be in tune, or watching the director. There are those, for purposes known only to themselves, who choose to sabotage the corporate hum. It may give them a perverse sense of power; so, they should have the opportunity to play their own tune somewhere else.

Have you experienced corporate hum in your workplace? In other settings?

What can you do to make this as frequent an experience as possible?

What makes it difficult for you to remove a discordant player?

Are there times when you should choose to sing in a different group?

It's a Murex Morning

"It's a beautiful morning…" I can almost hear the cheerful song as I walk the beach this morning. The wind and temperature are perfect and the beach is strewn with the lovely ribbed and pointed Apple Murexes. While not rare here, they are not common to many beaches.

People who live along the beach are carrying their coffee and walking their dogs. They are more intent on greeting neighbors and the new day than really looking for shells. Taking in the fresh air and the vistas makes an inspiring start to the day.

Benjamin Franklin, in his *Autobiography*, exhorted himself and others to "rise and greet the new day" – and to do it with energy, praise, and thanksgiving.

What small ritual can you build into your early morning to capture this spirit of exultation?

What could be done in your workplace to enhance the mood and productivity?

On military installations worldwide, the national anthem is played as the flag is raised (usually at a time when many are reporting for duty). If folks are outside, they come to attention facing the nearest flag – a good reminder of their noble mission as they start the new day. (A few of us even sing along!)

Lord of
All I Survey!

An amusing sight this afternoon – a Sandpiper had laid claim to a particularly fancy sand castle and was standing on the highest turret. King of the Mountain is a natural game played by animals, children, and many "adults."

Instead of "one-upsmanship," ... let's give the game a positive spin:

I want to see as far as I can see.

I want to acknowledge that I do own my perspective and interpretation of what I see.

And please, in the future, address me as "Lord Sandpiper!"

Balance of Action and Contemplation

People often ask me if I would like to move to Sanibel Island, or at least own a spot where I could go more frequently. So far, I tend to reply, "Then I would have to do laundry!" I would have to pollute my contemplative time with the mundane.

When I was a school teacher, I loved my summers "off" to travel and read all of those books I couldn't get to while grading students' work during the school year. But, about two weeks before the beginning of school, I began to anticipate the new classes and new approaches I could share. I was refreshed, reinvigorated, and eager to be active doing what I loved most.

Finding the right balance between the contemplative and active portions of our life is key and it changes with our ages and stages.

How can you find the right balance?

If you had a nine-month sabbatical, how would you use it?

Even on family vacations, how can you ensure contemplative time?

On a weekly basis, how can you ensure contemplative time?

When taking vacations, don't just do the mini-vacation so popular with working folks. Ensure that at least annually you have one long enough to really wind down.

Alpha and Beta Waves

One of the great benefits of a protracted vacation at the beach (or anywhere else) is that it gives us an opportunity to slow down our Beta Waves (the doing right now short wave activity) for the longer wave intuitive, subconscious explorations of the Alpha State.

I used to measure how stressed I was in my workplace by how many days it took me to reach the overwhelming yawns and the must-stop-on-the-beach-to-write-down-that-thought state. Then, I knew I was so relaxed that it would be unkind to expect my brain to hold that thought all of the way back to the cabin (maybe another hour and a half). I needed to clear that thought so that there was room for another. A pad of paper was a critical tool.

It is the same story in the middle of the night after you have tasked your brain with directed dreaming or problem-solving. When you awake and decipher your scribbles, you must reality test and then put into practice those Alpha contributions that you deem worthwhile.

One caution: you might want to be careful about describing your inspiration or handing your night time hieroglyphics to your secretary for decoding unless you are working with people who appreciate these strategies!

When have you experienced major breakthrough ideas?

How can you nurture yourself to enable further explorations?

Tracks
and Their Tales

The beach records the way we impact it, leaving our tracks in the sand. Some who are running barefoot, leave only the print of the ball of their feet and toes. Others, in heavy sports shoes, leave deep full-foot patterns.

Those in beach shoes leave only the outer outline of their shoe and barely an indent at all. Those walking barefoot rarely leave a print.

It is a thrill to walk on an isolated beach early in the morning and find the huge, but delicate tracks of a Great Blue Heron. Knowing that he has been there before me adds mystery and grandeur to the site, even though I have not seen him.

All of the prints are evanescent, apparent only to those who come before the next wave or the next tide. In spite of our concern with the immediate consequences of our actions, time erases most rather quickly.

So, our choice of the trail we leave impacts us more than anyone else.

How can this be instructive?

If you have blazed trails in your work, how do you ensure their continued existence and use?

In order not to close on a too existentially negative note, there are "tracts in the sand" — such tracts as Anne Morrow Lindbergh's *Gift from the Sea* and the U. S. Wildlife Refuges honoring J. N. "Ding" Darling and the Bailey family for their lasting contributions to the islands' wildlife.

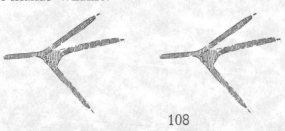

A Junonia and Lion's Paw Day!

Can you believe it? I found these two rare treasures within minutes of each other on what had appeared to be a rather unexceptional beach – until then! I had no expectations. I was really focused on finding perfect little "tuckers" to complete my design. (Somehow, I am always drawn to the big shells first and must force myself to find these small gems that become so critical at the completion of my projects.)

These two "stars" will deserve their own place of honor, not just be added to my pretty wreath or mirror frame. They need to be where I will see them often and be reminded that they are valued not only for their beauty, but also for their rarity.

They should be where others can see them, so that the wonder and pleasure can be shared. Maybe others will be inspired to seek them as well.

To put this day of double delight into perspective, I had found only one perfect Lion's Paw in the last decade. I had never found a Junonia. While I had told myself that finding one wasn't so important, my elation today belies my rationalization!

I also sense a little bit of the Chinese "never-finish-your-house" syndrome, which prophesies that when you finish your goal or dream, you will die. However, I never intended to measure my life's success by the one goal of finding a Junonia, so I do not think I am in serious jeopardy.

Have you had the exhilarating experience of not one, but two remarkable accomplishments in a short time frame? How did they happen?

Could your Junonia and Lion's Paw be exceptional people that you have encountered?

How can you keep the delight they brought into your life on a regular basis?

Keeping the Beach Alive on a Daily Basis

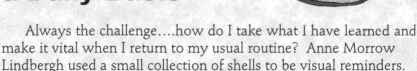

Always the challenge….how do I take what I have learned and make it vital when I return to my usual routine? Anne Morrow Lindbergh used a small collection of shells to be visual reminders.

J. Anthony Lukas, a guest instructor at the Wesleyan Writers Workshop just after winning his second Pulitzer Prize, met a young journalist's query of the same ilk. He suggested that the class could keep a small diagram right at eye level above the computer. Admitting that pressures to follow the traditional formula and spit out stories rapid-fire were not conducive to award-winning writing, he hoped we would choose one of the graphic winners he had shared with us.

You can use your office space as a gallery of fun – triggers to inspire you and those who visit you. Why not feature photos you have taken, a fishing rod or a poured resin box of fishing flies, or a hat rack of favorite caps or hats? The last could be especially useful when you are struggling with the budget! (Studies of creativity show that hats are incredible short cuts to your right brain. Most of us rely too heavily on our left brain and need conduits to our more innovative side.)

Surely your desk could use a sand bucket or two, or a glass lamp filled with specimens from the beach. A tape of ocean sounds might be just the right tonic when office conversations become intrusive. A little "Skin-so-Soft" or Citronella? Scent is a powerful reminder.

What triggers could you put in your work place to enhance your creativity and serve as conversation starters with co-workers or clients?

How frequently should you change them to avoid ennui?

Could you create your own equivalent of the Green Flash sunset ritual?

When is My Design Complete?

How do I know when my creative balance has been achieved? How do I know when it is time to start a new project?

This can be a hard question to answer. Some resist drawing any undertaking to a close, fearing that they do not know what, if anything, will come next. Others are eager to finish this project so that they can try something new. Some would prefer the recipe-driven menu, so that there are no surprises, for good or ill.

But, in the spirit of the beach, where each wave brings something new (different, if not better or worse), we need to have our own inner gyroscope, our own aesthetic sense developed over a lifetime. Then, we need to listen to it.

Once you ask the question, you are already considering closure. So, the issue becomes **When?** Reassess your abstract measures of your design and listen to your intuition – this is enough.

It will never be perfect, but is it appealing and feels right as it is? Then, examine your product, smile, and let it go.

What has been your experience with completion and new beginnings?

Must you ensure a new project before closing out an old one?

And the Greatest Gift...

is being alive and walking on the beach!

Do so intentionally, mindfully, delightfully every single day. Even when you are very far away geographically, you can task your brain to take you there.

No need to make reservations.

No need for a travel agent or a guide.

No waiting in crowded airports or in lines of traffic.

No cost.

You're there... sun on your back, waves lapping at your toes, and shells to explore...

Postlogue: Everywoman

I came to this beach six years ago, freshly retired from full time employment, a modified-radical mastectomy, and a radical chemotherapy regimen. My hair wasn't quite long enough for public display, but on the beach I could wear a sunhat instead of my wig.

Returning to a place that I loved to find the emotional and physical energies that I needed to survive, I relished long walks with my husband and long walks alone. Both versions supplied needed renewal.

I have thought about this a lot this year because a number of salespeople in Sanibel galleries and stores have said, "Don't I know you?" While my first reaction is to think that a lot of us my age probably look alike, the intensity in the queries has been puzzling.

As a much younger woman, my duple (as close to exact as seems possible with a stranger, not a twin) was the face on Pepsi ads and the model beside sailboats in classy magazines. Friends sent me these and said, "So this is what you do when the submarine is at sea!"

Do I look like Everywoman to these discerning artists and saleswomen? Is there an eye contact and approachability that enables these reactions? I hope so, because this book is every woman's story (and, I can dare to hope, every man's).

See you on the beach!

About the Author:
Kathleen Parker O'Beirne

What are the ingredients for thinking and writing about leadership?

Army daughter of a general, diplomat, writer and home economics teacher mother

Creek explorer and beach walker since age 8

"Friendship Queen" – 9th grade, after move #8, Junction City, KS

Smith College (B.A.) and Wesleyan University (M.A.L.S.)

Navy wife of a submariner and mother of two cherished children

Girl Scout and Scout leader for 7 troop years

Associate Editor, *Family Magazine* for 12 years

Public Affairs Officer and Program Manager (for spouse employment and volunteer management), Department of Defense Office of Family Policy and Support and Public Affairs Officer, Naval Underwater Systems Center, New London, CT

Director, Navy Family Service Center, Naval Submarine Base, New London, CT

Teacher/Instructor: junior high through university post-graduate levels (including the National Defense University)

Boards of Directors: USO World Board, Alumnae Association of Smith College, Southeastern CT Women's Network, Military Child Education Coalition, & Community Coalition for Children

Leadership Awards: Navy Wife of the Year, Outstanding Woman of the Year (both Camden County, GA BPW and S.E. CT Women's Network), Department of the Navy Meritorious Civilian Service Award, Athena Award, and United Church of Christ CT "Recognized Woman"

Re-order Information:

Life Is a Beach: Musings from the Sea
(ISBN 1-879979-09-8) $14.95

Birds of a Feather: Lessons from the Sea
(ISBN 1-879979-02-0) $19.95
Postage and handling per book: $ 2.00

Order by check or invoice to:
> Lifescape Enterprises
> P. O. Box 218
> West Mystic, CT 06388

Queries to:
phone (860) 536-7179
fax (860) 536-2288
email: kathleenobeirne@aol.com

Credit card purchases:
To use your credit card, contact your local book store or
> Bank Square Books Ltd (860) 536-3795
> (49 W. Main St., Mystic, CT 06355)
> Banksquarebks@msn.com